PRAISE FOR LAURIE NOTARO

Spooky Little Girl

"A comedic killer ... Notaro crafts a wondrously realistic afterlife. ... She is able to make death laughable in a heartfelt way."
—*Bust*

"A crazy, funny version of the afterlife."
—*Minneapolis Star Tribune*

"A novel that is full of laughter ... [Notaro] has a winner with this hilarious take on the joys and sorrows of the 'surprised demised.'"
—ChronWatch

"A fun story that mixes [Notaro's] unique humor with a sweet paranormal tale of friendship, family, and unfinished business."
—BookBitch

"Pure, unexpurgated Notaro ... Again [she] turns on the truth serum, and the results once more are riotously funny. ... *Spooky Little Girl* is a great summer beach read. The freshness it brings to a tired idea in chick lit—girl loses everything and exacts revenge by making herself over—is, well, refreshing."
—*San Antonio Express-News*

"An amazing story."
—*Seattle Post-Intelligencer*

"We're always thrilled to know that the prolific scribe of *Autobiography of a Fat Bride: True Tales of a Pretend Adulthood* and *We Thought You Would Be Prettier: True Tales of the Dorkiest Girl Alive* will crack us the you-know-what up with a new book just when we're casting about for something to read."　　　　　—*Phoenix New Times*

The Idiot Girl and the Flaming Tantrum of Death

"Hilarious."　　　　　—*Seattle Post-Intelligencer*

"[Laurie Notaro] writes with a flair that leaves you knowing she would be a gal you could commiserate with over a bucket of longneck beers. If you need to laugh over the little annoyances of life, this is a book for you. If you need to cry over a few of them, *Flaming Tantrum* can fit that bill, too."　　　　　—*St. Louis Post-Dispatch*

"A double-handful of chuckle-worthy vignettes . . . Notaro blends sardonic, often self-deprecating comedy with disarming sincerity."　　　　　—*Publishers Weekly*

"For pure laugh-out-loud, then read-out-loud fun, it's hard to beat this humor writer."　　　—New Orleans *Times-Picayune*

There's a (Slight) Chance I Might be Going to Hell

"[Notaro's] quirky humor, which she's previously showcased in her cult-classic essays on girly dorkdom, runs rampant."　　　　　—*Bust*

ALSO BY LAURIE NOTARO

Spooky Little Girl

The Idiot Girl and the Flaming Tantrum of Death

There's a (Slight) Chance I Might Be Going to Hell

An Idiot Girl's Christmas

We Thought You Would Be Prettier

I Love Everybody (and Other Atrocious Lies)

Autobiography of a Fat Bride

The Idiot Girls' Action-Adventure Club

It Looked Different on the Model

It Looked Different on the Model

EPIC TALES OF IMPENDING SHAME AND INFAMY

LAURIE NOTARO

VILLARD TRADE PAPERBACKS
NEW YORK

It Looked Different on the Model is a work of nonfiction.
Some names and identifying details have been changed.

A Villard Books Trade Paperback Original

Copyright © 2011 by Laurie Notaro

All rights reserved.

Published in the United States by Villard Books,
an imprint of The Random House Publishing Group,
a division of Random House, Inc., New York.

Library of Congress Cataloging-in-Publication Data
Notaro, Laurie.
It looked different on the model: epic tales of impending shame and infamy /
Laurie Notaro.
p. cm.
ISBN 978-0-345-51099-0 (pbk.)—ISBN 978-0-345-52631-1 (ebook)
1. Notaro, Laurie.   2. American wit and humor.   3. Humorists, American—21st
century—Biography.   4. Young women—Humor.   I. Title.
PS3614.O785Z474 2011
814'.6—dc22   2011002205

Printed in the United States of America

www.villard.com

4 6 8 9 7 5 3

To Heather, Haley, Ryan, and Hilary
Love, love, love

Contents

It Looked Different
on the Model

Let It Bleed

~

T he shirt was so pretty.

It had a little Peter Pan collar, and lining the placket were pintucks down the front, which were then framed by delicate little ruffles. The short puffed sleeves were like no other I had ever seen, almost Victorian but very casual and breezy. It was absolutely adorable.

So I went ahead and made mistake #1:

I picked up the price tag, which revealed a nugget of information that made my heart skip a beat—it was on sale. And while I could easily qualify for a conservatorship based on my math skills alone, I can divide stuff in half and am right almost 60 percent of the time, and in this case, that was dangerous enough for me to move on to mistake #2:

I imagined myself in it.

Of course, my imagination stars Laurie Circa 1994 and not Present-Day Laurie. Laurie Circa 1994, it also bears mentioning, is a Frankenstein-y hybrid of box-office movie posters and "Who Wore It Better" photos from *Us* magazine, which my mother appears to have a lifetime subscription to. This fantastical altered image consists of Uma Thurman's *Pulp Fiction* figure, Andie MacDowell's *Four Weddings and a Funeral* hair, and a Julia Roberts *I Love Trouble* smile. She not only looks cute in everything, she looks adorable. Laurie Circa 1994 also pictured herself in fifteen years as an editor at some hip magazine, high-powered enough to negotiate in her hiring package for her own bathroom that was complete with password activation and soundproofing. She never truthfully saw herself eating a fiber bar and a questionable banana for lunch right after checking to see if the whitehead on her nose had come back or if the yard guy would see her in her workout clothes, complete with her "Workin' for the Weekend" headband, which she felt forced to apologize for. Laurie Circa 1994 would have been disappointed that Present-Day Laurie, in the course of a workday, would easily be obsessed trying to outbid "ChuckyPup" on eBay for a pink dog parka; would scrawl notes that say, "Your car alarm goes off constantly and is irritating to those who work at home and pay taxes on this street. Park somewhere else; and your car, by the way, is a stupid color. Who would buy a yellow car? *Who?* It looks like you drive a huge banana." and stick them on the windshield of a particularly annoying Kia; or, for that matter would ever spend three consecutive hours looking in the mirror while employing six different sources of light trying to find one fugitive jowl hair. Things haven't exactly turned out the way Laurie Circa 1994 planned, even though, to Present-Day Laurie's benefit, if I feel like going to the bathroom at 2:30 P.M., I can do it with the door open should I prefer, although the potential to set off a car alarm is vastly upsetting.

In my head, Laurie Circa 1994 looked adorable enough in this shirt to actually brighten the day of not only herself but of everyone around her, in those puffy sleeves, pintuck details, and slight, flirty ruffles. And with that vision in mind—as Uma Thurman's body walked down the street, accompanied by a dog in a pink parka, and Andie MacDowell's hair bounced and glistened with shine in the sun, people turning and staring in her wake—Laurie Circa 1994 smiled to all, so cute in her ruffled shirt but *so humble* about it, her smile spread across her face, showing as many of Julia Roberts's teeth as would fit into her head, which was roughly about half.

And with that, I made mistake #3:

I pulled the shirt off the rack and asked if I could try it on. To be honest, I was already in over my head. The boutique was very nice, and I had admired its windows for months but had never caught it on an open day. When my luck had changed, I took the two steps into the store and did a quick sweep with all five senses, noticing a) mannequins so tiny I swear a bony sternum was impressed into them; b) the piping in of music overhead I couldn't possibly identify; and c) the presence of the lovely, exquisite creature positioned behind the front counter, who politely said hello with a French accent. I already knew by the international greeting *Bonjour!* that I was in the wrong space—I was the wrong size and wrong age and had the wrong wallet—but it was too late for me to turn around and swim back upriver to Elastic Land. Instead, I pressed on with the attitude that "I'm smaller than I look in real life," and I scanned the first rack with interest. I found myself picking at a hangnail because of my quick discomfort, which is a nervous habit that I understand isn't publicly acceptable, but if faced with a choice of thumb-sucking or fiddling with my crotch, I'll eat my cuticles any day. It was there that not only did I discover that the clothes were just as beautiful as I had seen in the window but that my size, indeed, was on the tags and, most important, on the tag of the cute shirt.

"Of course I'll show you to a dressing room," Amelie said as she walked out from the behind the counter and gave me a warm, real smile. Not only did all of Julia Roberts's teeth fit into her mouth, but they were *whiter*.

It was a cute dressing room—full-length mirror, a nice antique chair to put my purse on, and beautiful lighting. I like that, I thought as I looked into the mirror, noting that during my most recent visit to Anthropologie, the lights were so audacious I wanted to ask the dressing-room girl if she could turn the setting down from its current "Cruel" to the next level, "Barbaric." Now, I know I spent over half of my life puffing on a cigarette filter, but the Kitten Ass around my lips in my reflection at Anthropologie was so pronounced it looked like I had been injected with plasticine as I was sucking on a crack pipe. If you've never smoked, used a straw, or are still able to wear red lipstick without it spreading out like tributaries from your lips, you might not know that Kitten Ass is the nice term for the vertical fault lines that surround your mouth, and if you've never had a kitten, I suppose Puppy Ass would do. I refuse to take this conversation any further if you've never been a dog person, either, since I do not know what a ferret's ass looks like.

In the Anthropologie mirror, I saw wrinkles, dents, flaps, bumps, and something that caused me to say to myself, "I hope that's a tumor and not a horn." I was nothing short of horrified. As I sunk to the depths of despair and looked up the address of the closest cosmetic surgeon before I even left the dressing room, I tried in a panic to calm down.

"Every wrinkle you see is a wisdom line," I told myself in a nice, steady voice. "Wear them proudly; each one is a challenge and an obstacle you have triumphed over."

"You have an asshole *on your face*," one of my meaner voices replied. "Doesn't everyone want a juicy Wisdom Kiss from that mouth?"

"You're just growing into your face," the nice voice said. "There is grace in aging."

"Especially if you ever wanted to use your face as a baseball glove," the mean voice countered. "It gets softer and more doughlike."

"You know, these lights are ridiculously bright and are shining on you from directly up above," the nice voice tried again. "When does that ever happen in a real-life setting?"

"I dunno," the mean voice said in a mocking tone. "Ever hear of *the sun*?"

As a result of that experience, I do think all Anthropologies should provide a courtesy volcano just outside their dressing rooms so every woman who is revealed as completely inadequate by the lighting can throw herself in rather than contaminate the store staging for any longer than absolutely necessary.

But the lighting in this boutique was soft, welcoming, almost loving. Looking in the mirror, I swore there was a sheet of delicate gauze separating me and my reflection; I almost looked as blurry as a main character on *Dynasty*.

"I am perfect," my nice voice whispered.

"I bet you have glaucoma," my mean voice whispered back.

In any case, the conditions were prime for me to take the little ruffled shirt and try it on, and that's just what I did. I hung it up on an old antique hook on the wall and admired it briefly. And that's when I saw it: the "M" on the tag in the back of the shirt where the "L" rightfully should have been.

My heart made the sound of a deflating balloon. "Why, why?" it cried, like it had gotten whacked in the knee with a police baton at a practice for the U.S. Figure Skating Championship. I looked at the price tag, which did say "L," and realized it had just been mis-tagged. I was about to give the whole thing up when I saw the sale price again and thought that I might as well give it a shot. After all, what is the difference between an "M" and an "L," anyway? A boob size? Several good meals in a row? A couple weeks of unemployment?

So I did it. I jumped in, took the ruffled blouse off the hanger, and slipped it on. All was going well until I slipped my second arm in and we reached what I like to call "the friction point" of my arms, which is the upper portion right around the biceps area. After all, I'm pretty strong, so the circumference naturally reflects that, plus that's where I store most of my winter reserves, which should save me if I'm ever floating out in the ocean on a raft and my foot begins to look like a delicious burrito. But it was no big deal. I met some resistance, but with a little tug here and a little tug there, the sleeves moved right into place and the shirt was over my shoulders and on its way to being buttoned.

But it turns out that there sort of is a significant difference between an "M" and an "L," kind of like the difference between 1994, a decade's worth of unemployment, and the cultivation of a Kitten Ass. I couldn't even get the button and the hole to look at each other, let alone kiss. There was no bridging the mountain range—it was a statistically impossible feat, and one that was difficult to absorb. I really loved that shirt. I wanted to wear it. But it was a hard fact of life, a tragedy of reality you have to accept, like the fact that you can seriously injure your mouth by attempting to fit an entire Triscuit inside it, and your chances of bleeding don't diminish the more times you do it.

I looked at myself in it, saw Laurie Circa 1994 donning it with a cute little flippy skirt and espadrilles, and then bid it adieu. I slipped it off one shoulder, then the other, and that was precisely when our goodbye came to an abrupt end.

I was stuck. The sleeves, which had perfectly popped into

place with two teeny suggestive tugs, were now a little stubborn about leaving their nice, soft, cozy arm-fat nest. In fact, both refused to budge. I rolled my eyes and huffed at the inconvenience. I decided to pop them right back out of place with a tug downward and crossed the left hand behind me to grab the right placket of the shirt, and vice versa. One good solid tug.

Tug. *Tug. Tug.*

No movement. None at all. Not even a slide.

Now, when I say that the hems of the sleeves were firmly in place around my arms, I mean they came together like a pipe fitting. With a touch of plumber's putty, I could have run crude oil through that connection and there wouldn't have been the slightest chance of a leak.

And it was definite. Those puff sleeves weren't going anywhere.

I stood there for a moment and pondered what my next maneuver should be. Clearly we were having a little problem with the fabric of the shirt, which simply didn't have as much elasticity as it should have. Clearly. I mean, I have had to wiggle in and wiggle out of some items of clothing, sure, who hasn't, but I've never been *grafted* to one before.

I decided that since both of my arms were stuck and pulling from behind me wasn't working, I should try a different position, so I bent over and tried to grab the back of the shirt to pull it from that angle. I tried to grab it several times, but it was too tight across my shoulders to fall into my grasp, and I had been bent over so long that when I stood up I didn't see just stars but a meteor shower. "You'd better not do that again," I warned myself. "One more tip of the teapot and you'll come up with one side of your mouth lower than the other." I tugged again from the front, but the sleeves were decidedly not budging.

"How can you be trapped in a goddamned shirt?" I asked myself. "It's not a coal mine. It's not an elevator. It's *cotton*. The fabric of our lives!" I had no idea that a steel trap would have ruffles on it when I brought it into the dressing room and it sprang on both my arms.

"Oh my God," I whispered, then took a minute to refocus and pulled again.

Not. An. Inch.

"This is ridiculous," I said to myself. "I am just not pulling hard enough. Try pulling one arm at a time, focus all of your strength into one arm. Focusing. Focusing. Now pull!"

Something moved. But as my stomach flipped like a fish, I realized it was simply that the nail on my middle finger had bent backward.

If I get this shirt off, I thought, I swear I will never try on a non-"L" shirt again. Never. Never will I try to tempt sizes. Never will I think that sizes don't know what they're talking about. The sizes are gods. They know all. *They know all*. I know nothing. I'll stay in my size herd from now on and will never stray. There is safety in the herd.

I thought I could not only get an "M" on but that I could *button* it. I have learned my lesson. I have. I have. I promise I have. I'll only try things on with Lycra in them from now on. Never take on cotton straight. Never! *You always need a mixer! Now go in there and get that damned shirt off!*

I grabbed each side of the shirt with opposite hands, rolled my shoulders like I was Beyoncé, and pulled as very hard as I could. And I did it again, and again and again. I jumped up and down, trying to jar the shirt loose, I leaned down to the left and then down to the right, I wiggled, I shook, I shimmied, I even bent my knees and squatted for some unknown reason, all trying to pull that thing off. After several minutes, with a beet-red face and a mustache of sweat bubbles, I stopped and had to take a break and plopped down in the antique chair.

"I can't believe this," I whispered, my eyes closed. I was exhausted. Komodo dragons don't lock on to prey this hard.

"Honestly, why are you so fat?" even the nice voice inside my head asked me. To which I shook my head.

I don't know. I didn't know. *I just am.*

"Those arms are like tractor tires," the nice voice informed me. "They are so large they almost have their own gravitational pull! And you lied about being strong. That's not the reason they're so big. You just eat too many pretzels."

I totally deserved this, I realized. I deserved to get captured in this shirt. I was roped in like a calf. Stupid. So stupid. Just because it was on sale, I had to try on a baby shirt. This was so completely my fault. Maybe I should go to Baby Gap tomorrow and try to get into some Onesies or a romper. What was I thinking? Really? You know what's going to happen now? Firemen are going to have to come and cut me out of it, that's what. I hate this shirt, I don't like this shirt, and I don't want it anymore. It's not even a shirt, it's a straitjacket. A straitjacket with preposterous puff sleeves *that just make my arms look fatter surrounded by fat clouds.*

I looked so stupid. Sitting there. Sweating. Out of breath. Shirt hanging open like a domestic abuser's after a NASCAR race. I just wanted to go home and eat pretzels and Google "Why do intestines gurgle?" I prayed there were no security cameras in here, because I knew if there were, the video— twenty minutes straight of a topless fat lady looking like she was fighting Freddy Krueger in a dressing room—was going to outdo Susan Boyle, David After Dentist, and any guy getting rammed in the nuts with a baseball bat or golf club in YouTube history.

I sighed. All right, fine, I agreed, nodding to the universe. I'm in a shirt I can't get out of, or one I'll never get out of alive, anyway. Someday they'll find me in here, the jaw of my skeleton hanging open, my bra exposed and dripping off my rib cage, the sleeves of the shirt floating ethereally around my humerus bones now that there was no permafat to keep them in place like handcuffs.

I need a nap. I'm so tired. Done fighting. I give in. Shirt wins.

"You win, shirt," I whispered, just to make it official. "You win."

And as I looked in the mirror at myself—a half-naked woman, completely defeated—I understood now. The "friction point" was evidently the event horizon after all, and once I passed that mark there was just no going back. In a second, I'd be redshifted, stuck here forever, looking a little too much like the captain in *WALL-E* for my liking. But then I noticed something in the mirror under the gracious lighting, and for a moment, I saw Laurie Circa 1994 looking great in the shirt, her little Uma Thurman arms so nice in the loose sleeves, the placket buttoned without any bulging gaps from top to bottom.

She smiled her Julia Roberts smile at me, I smiled back, and softly she gave me a look of sympathy. But then the smile quickly vanished and she stared me straight in the eye.

"Get out of that goddamned shirt right now," she fired quickly. "You look like an asshole just sitting there. *You* got it on; *you* get it off. Don't you dare give up! You rip that shirt off if you have to!"

And she was right, or maybe I was just rested, I don't know, but my sweat mustache had finally dried up and I thought that maybe, yes, I could give it another shot. I stood up, and without any hesitation I went back in and pulled and fought and yanked, and suddenly the sleeves both popped free and the shirt slid down to my wrists.

I got that thing off me as fast as I could and put it back on the hanger on the wall before it could reattach itself to my body. It was so wrinkled it looked like a dishrag, and no wonder with all of the tugging and pulling that had been going on. Then I saw a speck of something on the hem of the shirt, perhaps some lint or a thread, but it did not move when I brushed it off. I immediately saw another, next to a button, and another on the bodice, and yet another on the inside of the shirt. All were red, and none were coming off. And the more I looked, the more I found, all over the shirt: inside, out, up and down, some dots, some smudges, and then a streak across the front hem. How had I not noticed this when I pulled it off the sales rack? It was very obvious that there was something all over this shirt, even if you weren't looking at it carefully.

I pulled it closer to my eyes to see if I could figure out what it was, and it was then that I made a match. The red streaks and smudges all over this shirt matched the middle finger on my left hand, which—despite the fact that the circulation to my arms had been severed for the last twenty minutes—was bleeding like a Halloween prop from the hangnail I had picked at. I don't know if I have arteries behind my nails or if I had moved around so much that I actually raised my heart rate to a healthy pace, but I had decimated this poor shirt so badly it looked like a Manson family member had worn it. A lot. To both houses. My struggle with the piece of clothing was now documented forever, my epic battle smeared all over the once-adorable shirt. No wonder I got all dizzy when I bent over, I realized. I lost a pint of blood in that fight! There was still no way I could present a bloody shirt to Amelie and then hand over my credit card with a smile and not have her push a panic button under the counter to alert authorities. So I got myself together, put my shirt that I could actually close back on, and walked out of the dressing room.

"How did you do?" Amelie asked, still sporting a pleasant smile.

"Oh," I said, smiling back. "This shirt pretty much captivated me!"

"It's so cute," she agreed. "I couldn't believe it went on sale that much!"

"I know!" I said enthusiastically, and walked back over to the sales rack.

Frankly, I had no idea how I was going to get the shirt back on the rack without Amelie noticing that I had finger-painted it with body fluids, because that really was my first plan: Get it back on the rack and get out of the store. But after a moment I realized that you don't try on a pair of pants, fart in them, and then put them back on the shelf, and the same rough politeness boundaries applied here, too. Plain and simple, I bled on it, I bought it.

So I picked up a little frilly slip I saw on the sales rack, too—also, duly noted, an "M" (there's no such thing as an "L" on sale in a skinny-girl store, I am beginning to learn)—put it in front of the shirt, then walked the both of them back to the counter where Amelie stood, waiting.

"Oh, and a slip, too?" she said, to which I nodded again and laid them both on the counter, the slip on top and the tags for both visible.

"You know what? You can fold them up together, save on tissue paper," I offered.

I didn't want her handling the shirt any more than she needed to.

"And I don't need a bag, either," I added, just to make sure she didn't come in contact with any of my DNA.

As I walked out of the store with my new tiny baby clothes in hand, I knew that, after all of that, the shirt was really the cutest thing ever, but it was still also an "M," so in my book it sorta deserved what it got for messing with a big girl. Like Present-Day Laurie.

Who had just bought herself a brand-new, bloodstained, size "M" ruffly shirt after the toughest fight she'd ever had.

She's a Pill

As soon as I saw the red envelope fall through the mail slot, I knew something was amiss. But it wasn't until I tore the perforated edge and slid the envelope out of the mailer that I knew she had struck again.

"Oh no!" I whined, loud enough to prompt my husband to come running and entered the room with a worried look on his face.

"What is it?" he said quickly.

I extended my arm and stomped my foot as he took it from my hand.

"*Precious*!" he exclaimed, reading the title. "*Based on the Novel 'Push' by Sapphire*! You're kidding. I thought you said you weren't going to let her get on Netflix anymore."

"You know I can't control her," I said quietly. "I think getting *Zack and Miri Make a Porno* in the mail last week more than proves that. She's an entity unto herself. She does what she likes; I have nothing to do with it."

"You need to get ahold of this," my husband said, shaking the envelope. "Because this is now out of hand. I was expecting *Battlestar Galactica* today. And now I get to spend Saturday afternoon playing Halo and watching *Precious*?"

"*Based on the Novel 'Push' by Sapphire*," I added.

"Set her straight, and do it now," my husband warned. "Before we get three copies of *Prince of Persia* in the mail."

"You don't have to watch it," I informed him.

"*Of course* you have to watch it!" he protested. "If you don't watch it, you've asked the mailman to walk up to your house and back for nothing. And that's just sadistic. I *hate* her."

"Hate is a strong word," I reminded him. "She doesn't hate you."

"Oh yeah?" he replied snidely, and held up the red envelope. "What's this?"

I understood my husband's anger, but, I mean, after all, it wasn't me who put *Precious* on the list. *She* did.

Now, I will admit that she can be somewhat of a handful, but no one has experienced the consequences of her actions with as much interest as I have. Imagine, if you will, me waking up in a hotel room in New York, getting out of bed, and having my bare feet land in a nest of something crunchy that attacked my body quickly and with a forceful bond, like leeches. That's exactly what happened to me before I shuffled to the bathroom and I realized I had a multitude of sticky cellophane wrappers affixed to my feet and ankles, and one particularly skilled wrapper with amazing climbing talents had made it up to my calf.

Initially, I was stunned and concluded that some hotel employee with a weird wrapper fetish and who liked to watch fat ladies sleep had been in my room the night before, opening DVDs and things from Costco by the side of my bed. But on closer inspection, I noticed that each wrapper had a residue on it—gummy, dense, and bright white. I recognized it immediately. It was frosting, and my suspicions were confirmed when I inspected one of the gummy patches closer and saw what could be nothing but the grooves of tongue tracks.

Oh, I thought shamefully. I know that tongue. The wide, overreaching lick and misshapen taste buds due to obscene amounts of salt intake. *I know that tongue!!* When I looked in the mirror, I saw proof positive. There had been no fetishist in the room, unwrapping box sets of Ken Burns documentaries and baby wipes. Nope. On my face was a five o'clock shadow consisting of Devil Dog crumbs from a box of snack cakes I had planned to mail my father later that morning. Suddenly, flashes of the ravage popped into my head. Actually, I don't think it was as much of a ravage as it was a chubby girl sitting in bed in a dark room, eating snack cakes one after the other as crumbs fell out of her mouth and she threw the wrappers to the floor after she was done licking them, using both hands. Truth be told, it's the same scene in broad daylight, except more people would be repulsed. And children would be told to look away.

The next morning, I shuffled out of the bathroom shortly after waking up and decided that the shoes I had seen on a website the day before definitely needed purchasing. I'd had dreams I was wearing them and was subsequently told by others in my reverie that the shoes "made my toes look quite thin." Frankly, if anyone—real or otherwise—is seeing a shoe mirage that shows bones in my feet, I don't care if there's a squeak toy at the end of the big curled-up toe and a big red puff on them: Those shoes will be on my piggies by sundown.

Now determined to secure them, I flipped open my laptop, and my computer screen went immediately to my email account, which showed me that at a little after midnight the night before, a receipt arrived.

A receipt for shoes that, according to my imaginary friends, made my toes appear starved.

This has to be a mistake, I thought to myself; I didn't buy

those shoes last night. I know I looked at those shoes but didn't buy them. I am fairly sure that I didn't buy shoes last night; how can you buy shoes without putting in a credit-card number? Wow. Look at that. At 12:13 A.M. last night I bought shoes, evidenced by the last four digits of my credit-card number right there on the email receipt, under "payment method."

I concluded that I must have clicked a button I didn't intend to click, and, really, I was going to buy the shoes anyway, so was it that big a deal that I accidentally bought them?

And my plan was to recount just that to my best friend, Jamie, when I called her later that day.

"This is crazy, but last night I saw a pair of shoes online that I loved," I began. "They were these super cute red—"

"Open-toed slingbacks with white stitching," she finished for me. "I know, I was on the phone with you when you bought them."

"You . . . *what*?" I said very slowly.

"Yeah, you said that if you got them," she continued, "you would even cut and paint your nails, including the patches of skin on those couple of toes where your toenails fell off and never grew back because you tried shoes on without socks in a thrift store in 1987."

"I told you about those fallen toenails?" I cried, almost hyperventilating.

"Everyone knew why you wore cowboy boots in a-hundred-twenty-degree weather," she informed me. "No one believed you were allergic to the rubber in flip-flops."

"I still don't understand when it was that I talked to you," I said, trying to piece together the events of the night prior. "What time did you call?"

"No, no, no, my friend," Jamie said. "I guess *you* called *me* at around nine."

"I called *you*? Which made it midnight my time," I concluded. "How long did we talk?"

"Long enough to plot out the entire strategy of my divorce proceedings," she said. "So far, you decided that we're going to retain Gloria Allred, have a press conference on TMZ, and then you gave me a voodoo spell to make his teeth fall out."

"Does it involve lemons, a black candle, and something called cursing oil?" I asked suspiciously.

"As a matter of fact it does," Jamie confirmed.

"In my dream, that's what I used on my feet to make the toes shrink," I said.

"Nope," Jamie corrected me. "Makes your teeth fall out. We'll know for sure in three to six weeks."

"How long did we talk?" I asked.

"Long enough for you to take a trip to Hogwarts and then go shoe shopping," she said.

"This is crazy," I said. "I only remember part of it as a dream, but I don't remember talking to you at all."

"I'm not surprised," she said blankly. "You told me you had just taken an Ambien."

"Ooh," I cooed, as if I was talking about a cute baby or the surviving snack cake on the dresser. "I love Ambien. I slept all night. Didn't wake up once!"

"Or did you?" my best friend questioned. "Because if you did, you wouldn't know about it. Ambien gives you amnesia. Once you're out, you're out. People sleep-drive on that stuff and all sorts of other crazy things."

It was like Nixon calling Frost.

And, it turns out, some people get on their Netflix queues and then get movies in the mail after they've made statements like "I have no desire to see *Precious*, think *The September*

Issue is a far more socially relevant movie, and I don't care what that says about me as a person."

It turns out that with one pop of a little tiny pill, I unleash my id, also known as Ambien Laurie. Ambien Laurie, in more basic terms, is my raw monkey form. I don't really think she plots out her brand of chaos, it just naturally happens, like the formation of the universe. She can be unpredictable. She can be naughty. She can be earthy. I don't think she does it on purpose, much like monkeys don't wake up in the morning with plans to rip people's faces off; it sort of happens in the spur of the moment and if the time feels right. I've decided that Ambien is apparently kind of like taking a de-evolution pill, which shorts out the synapses and unwinds any social conventions already imprinted in the brain; for eight hours, I am nothing short of *Australopithecus* returning to the plains to hunt and gather, and if that means bringing back salty snack foods and snappy sandals to my bed, so be it.

After I realized I was turning into a nocturnal ape zombie who would rip the guts out of any snack cake within an arm's distance, had access to my credit card, and would delve into the kingdom of the dark arts with little to no provocation, I weighed the odds. And, I'm sorry, there was just no contest. I like sleeping, so if a Twinkie or Devil Dog had to die every now and then at the hands of a teeth-gnashing night-eater, I was cool with that. If a new pair of shoes popped up on my front porch every now and then, that was a thrill, and, I'm sorry, but I don't see how I lose in this game.

From what I can piece together, the de-evolution of myself to Ambien Laurie is fairly swift, and the entire transformation takes place within a single second. According to my husband, who has in fact seen her materialize, when Ambien Laurie takes charge, I become a very calm yet highly aggressive person, like a gunfighter, who looks at him with an expression that relays calmly, "Sure, go ahead and eff with me. I'll eat your face off. I'm cool, either way. You make the call."

To me, however, it goes almost unnoticed until the next day, when I might see what I believe is a shard of wood on the bathroom floor and panic, thinking we might have termites, until I pick it up, realize it is a pretzel, and my mind quickly flashes to Ambien Laurie sitting on the potty and shoving pretzels into her gullet like popcorn at 3:00 A.M. Or when walk into my office and see a cheese cracker sandwich delicately balanced on the corner of the hall table, and I have an immediate flashback of walking into the living room in the middle of the night, rooting through my purse like a truffle pig. I'm eating the twin of the cracker, instead of throwing them away because they were in my purse for the better part of a solstice, although Ambien Laurie filed that nugget of information away for later retrieval, when it was her feeding time. Or when I'm getting my morning coffee and the box of Triscuits is open and sitting on the counter, and I remember that I was standing there at three in the morning, looking at the Triscuit and then at an Oreo and thinking: I'll eat *this* now while I'm waiting to eat *that* cookie.

Ambien Laurie is also scientifically inclined, as evidenced by the memory of her responding to a dream in which my living-room wall was entirely covered, floor to ceiling, by a chart, much like the periodic table of elements. In each little box, however, was not a letter abbreviation but a number and a delightful drawing of what appeared to be distinct and different mushroom clouds, swirlies, and scrolls. In the dream, I was in awe of the complexity of the chart and all of the elaborate illustrations when my eyes finally reached the top and it all became clear: It was The Fart Chart (see pages 26–27), and every type of fart, categorized by its ferocity, attributes, bubbles, and bursts, was depicted in a very artistic rendering with a corresponding identification number.

Still swimming in the dream as she stumbled to the bathroom through the dark hallway, Ambien Laurie sat on her throne and thought to herself, Ahhh, number 248 is a good one. I should really do that one more often.

The evidence of Ambien Laurie is present not only in random crumbs around my house and bursts of nighttime brilliance but also in snippets of emails the next morning. I have woken up numerous mornings to find responses in my inbox to emails I was unaware I had sent from deep within the shadows of the previous evening, and I have to start piecing events together like it's a crime-scene investigation. Imagine my surprise when Ambien Laurie wove a tale about Mr. Grunt, a sixty-five-year-old phys ed teacher who was covered in graying marsupial fur and kept his hamburgers warm underneath his floppy man boobs. Yeah. I already know. If you think it was horrible reading that, imagine the horror of discovering you not only *wrote* it but *sent* it to people, and I mean people as in *plural*. Picture that the thought of Mr. Grunt actually emerged from your unconscious and that your self-edit button was not only deactivated but completely disconnected by a ravenous eater of purse trash, who then realized there was no one in the air-traffic-controller tower, thus allowing random and crazy-ass thoughts to fly out of the brain airport unattended, Mohamed Atta–style. You could write a story about lost Germanic children, a witch, and an oven, and you would get a softer response than from a story about Mr. Grunt, who really is a bastard. I had revealed a part of myself that I never wanted others to see, kind of like when Michael Kors took his shirt off on the beach and exposed his unholy, Pluto-sized flesh-covered belly button to millions of tabloid readers. If I could insert a link right here to that mind-burning image, I would, because it is perhaps the only thing revolting enough to divert your attention away from the shame that I conjured up a PE teacher who uses body flaps as a food warmer.

Perhaps the worst thing about this tale of caution is that most nights at around 10:00, 10:15 P.M., certain friends will knock on my email door and ask if Ambien Laurie can come out to play, and if I mention, no, she's not home, they'll reply very simply that they'll check back in forty-five minutes. They think she's hilarious, and, honestly, if you think a monkey eating your food, spending your money, and poaching your friends is the bottom rung, wait till those friends start clapping for her when she flings around the Mr. Grunt talk. Watch what happens then (Ambien Laurie said of the Kors belly button: "Someone's mother was a lazy piece of shit. She couldn't tie a string around that?"). Perhaps it could be worse; my friend Rick, after a night of restful, peaceful Ambien sleep, woke up and climbed out of bed, only to notice that his underwear, which had been on him when he climbed into bed half an hour after taking his pill, was gone. It remained a mystery until he left for work an hour later, when he found his briefs on the sidewalk that led to the garage.

So I suppose that she could be worse and get behind the wheel of a car, go on an all-you-can-eat binge at IHOP, or take a stroll around the neighborhood while leaving her panties behind in the driveway. Right? Things could be worse, right? I mean, essentially, Ambien is *you* in an altered state, kind of like the twilight sleep that women of my mother's generation were given when they went into labor. And, for that matter, I am thrilled that when I wake up all I find is pretzel shards on my bathroom mat or cookie crumbs on my face and not a bassinet next to my bed with an offspring in it who expects me to pay for college.

I just hope I don't have another nighttime family somewhere.

Whatever. Ambien Laurie is not so bad. She's really not. She's just active. Would it be better if she sat around, calling people to tell them that she loved them, like every average alcoholic? Bo-ring. Big deal. Who can't do that? Ambien Laurie is an innovator; she has taken the nighttime to a new level. So sometimes she eats on the potty. Who cares? It's basically like any other chair in the house, it just has more options.

I'm getting a little hungry. Feels like snack time. If I'm not mistaken, that remaining cheese cracker sandwich is still on the table in the hall. She talks big about throwing shit away; she never does, and of course I'm going to eat it. Of course I'm going to eat it!! But not all of it. I'll only eat half of it and leave the other half under her pillow. That'll get her all worked up.

Hey, Mr. Grunt. How's it goin'? Wanna watch *Precious*?

No, I don't wanna bite. Gotta cracker in the hall. Keep the burrito in your shirt, please.

Listen, we're not watching *Gran Torino* again. I hope that's not going to be a problem. 'Cause I'll eat your face off. I'm cool, either way.

You make the call.

The Fart Chart

Fig. 214
This Is MY Town

Origin: Grilled meat
Culprit: Cowboys, the bald, people who wear leather jackets
Habitat: Poker tables, Lincoln Continentals, deserted lots in New Jersey

Fig. 195
The Scream

Origin: Exotic cuisine, mostly unidentified, hooves, snouts
Culprit: MBAs, Olympic athletes, missionaries
Habitat: Hostels, brothels, China

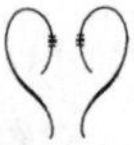

Fig. 381
The Gambler

Origin: Fast food
Culprit: Kenny Rogers, wrestling fans
Habitat: Trucks that weigh more than houses
Outstanding qualities: You gotta know when to hold 'em, fold 'em, know when to walk away and when to run

Fig. 335
Brown Egg

Origin: Sugar-free chocolates with maltitol
Culprit: Secretaries, insurance adjustors, teens
Habitat: Pampered chef parties, cubicles
Outstanding qualities: Danger is enormous in high-profile situations

Fig. 307
The Nail Gun

Origin: Doritos, mixture of domestic and imported beers, items of deep-fried nature
Culprit: Musicians, construction workers, Mormons
Habitat: Futons, under Mexican blankets, old carpeting

Fig. 333
Fiber One

Origin: Any product compressing 20% of daily fiber into a geometric shape
Culprit: Women in their 40s
Habitat: Crosswalks, TJ Maxx, elevators
Outstanding qualities: Is never alone; has many cousins trailing in packs

Fig. 171
Coward

Origin: Juicy Juice, Ritz Bits, Fruit Roll-Ups
Culprit: Babies, John Boehner, the comatose
Habitat: Car seats, hospice, tanning booths

Fig. 219
The Countess

Origin: Foie gras, canned meat, asparagus
Culprit: Aristocrats, porn stars, pirates
Habitat: High seas, dressing rooms, wine tastings, first class, on location in San Fernando Valley

Fig. 248
SOS

Origin: Bologna sandwiches, eggs prepared any way, generic sodas
Culprit: Enlisted men, evangelists
Habitat: Tight quarters, baggage claim

Fig. 274
The Monk

Origin: Soy products, gluten-free muffins, lactose-free yogurt
Culprit: All residents of Seattle
Habitat: Yoga class, Whole Foods
Outstanding qualities: Can emit three tones at once *with perfect pitch*

Fig. 459
The Zipper

Origin: Protein bars, excessive amounts of pork products
Culprit: Rock climbers, ex-boyfriends, trapped miners
Habitat: Caves, REI
Outstanding qualities: May cause physical damage if the culprit is sitting during transmission

Fig. 475
Mr. Grunt

Origin: Hot dogs, frozen burritos, fake crab
Culprit: Retirees, dead gym teachers
Habitat: Costco sample carts, will hover over the backs of couches, all public transportation

Fig. 345
Little Mouse

Origin: Cheese, particularly spray, boxed, or jarred
Culprit: Dogs, 7th-grade math teachers, uncles
Habitat: Teachers' lounge, comic-book stores, your pillow
Outstanding qualities: Easily translates to weaponry, bio and traditional

Fig. 346
Too Many Cherries

Origin: Overindulgence of dried or seasonal fruit
Culprit: Women of advancing age, romance writers, Nancy Pelosi
Habitat: Coffe shops, comfort shoe stores, J. Jill

Fig. 363
Hippie

Origin: Organic matter, unspecified
Culprit: Anyone dirty, poets, "peaceniks"
Habitat: Commonly found unattended at Burning Man, protests of any sort, bulk-food aisle.
Outstanding qualities: Scatters like buckshot with potential of up to a mile radius

The Post Office Lady with the Dragon Tattoo

~

I had been dreading this day for more than a year.

I felt my heartbeat speed up as I took another step forward in line, one customer closer and a few feet nearer to the counter. I kept my eyes down, focusing on the scrape on the top of my boot or on the collection of measuring cups and kitchen accessories that lined the aisle where I was trapped. I didn't want to look up. I couldn't even bring myself to try.

The Mean Lady might be looking at me.

Typically I don't have such anxiety while waiting in line at the post office, but, to tell the truth, I was on the verge of a panic attack. I was starting to sweat, and there was no doubt that I felt jittery to the point that I thought I might explode.

I cursed myself for not taking a Valium in preparation. I wasn't supposed to be here.

And the Mean Lady knew that.

I looked up quickly. She had her eyes locked on me like the infrared laser beam of an unmanned drone.

A wave of trepidation swallowed my body, especially my GI tract, and I felt the smothering desire to flee. I was almost ready to turn on my heels and head back out the door when I remembered the package in my arms, and a bolt of bravery hit me. No, it said. You must stay. You have things to mail for your little nephew, your little nephew who will only wear something referred to as "unders" briefs from a kids' store called Hanna Andersson, an outlet store of which just happens to be across the street from Jamie's house.

Do it for the boy, the bolt of bravery said. *Do it for the unders.*

So I stayed, despite the terror, despite the laser eyes, despite the consequences. When I walked into the store, I already knew my chances of making it up to the counter were as slim as my mother making it through a pregnancy without smoking.

When we first moved in to our house in Eugene, I used to enjoy going to our little post office satellite station, located inside the drugstore and stocked to meet literally any human need you might have within the bounds of the law. It has a garden section, pet department, party-goods area, several rows of greeting cards—in essence, it's a drugstore but with way more stuff hanging from the ceiling, stacked on the shelves, and popping out from the walls. It's not a place you want to go if you're averse to confined, cramped quarters or get easily embarrassed if you knock things down, because that's just part of the experience. I'm not sure how many people with OCD have spontaneously combusted in that store, but I'm sure the number is not insignificant. You walk in, wander through the labyrinth of sparkly Hello-Kittied hologrammed trinkets, topple over end caps, get lost, suddenly find yourself examining a condom with a pirate on it, and then attempt to claw your way back out by following hints of daylight. The store has a whole lotion department, packages of fake poo, hillbillies you can grow from a capsule, what some people would say is the largest collection of aging candy on the West Coast, and more Christmas villages than the European Union, including Turkey. It looks as if you took my bedroom in seventh grade and put price tags on everything. I truly am at a loss to explain it in all of its cataclysm, although my old friend Grace summed it up nicely by describing it as the "Best Place to Get Impaled by a Unicorn."

But I loved the fact that it had a post office, because it was so close by. At the time, I was sending out a lot of mail—stickers and magnets that I shipped off to Idiot Girls around the country—and had a backlog I needed to conquer from the months my stuff was in storage.

Unfortunately, during that lapse, the post office had a two-cent rate hike, which meant that I needed to invest in additional postage. I headed off to my new satellite post office inside the drugstore and waited at the end of a long, long line.

When it was my turn at the counter, I stepped up and smiled at the lady behind it.

She smiled back.

I needed four hundred two-cent stamps. So I asked for four hundred two-cent stamps.

The post office lady looked at me like I had just asked her if she wanted to buy my sex tape. In fact, she actually gasped.

"Oh, no," she told me, shaking her head vigorously. "I can't give you that. Absolutely not."

To be honest, I didn't say anything, because I didn't have anything to say. I did this all the time in Phoenix. One time I bought six hundred stamps, and the post office guy didn't even look at me, let alone challenge me to a standoff and act as if I had pantomimed a lewd gesture.

"So, wait," I replied, trying to process it, then a moment later arriving at the most obvious conclusion. "Oh, you don't have four hundred?"

"Sure I have four hundred," she replied. "But if I give you

four hundred, then there won't be as many left for the next person who wants two-cent stamps."

Again, I stood there for a moment, attempting to act like a Bounty paper towel and absorb. But it wasn't working. Asininity was puddling all around me in quantities too vast to soak up.

I tried to appeal to her work ethic as a government employee and replied, "Well, I have to mail out four hundred envelopes and I need four hundred stamps."

Without missing a beat, she churlishly snapped, "Well, you can't take them all for yourself! Someone else might need some, and if I give them all to you, then I have to order more from the post office."

"But you *are* the post office," I tried to reason, getting frustrated. "What does it matter if I take all four hundred or if I take two hundred and the guy behind me then asks for two hundred? You'll still have to order them."

Then the surly came out. "No," she informed me firmly. "I won't do it. I'll give you two hundred and that's all. You can't have them all. No."

Quickly I weighed my options, which I quickly discovered were none. Our negotiations had hit a wall, and I was well aware that I possessed less than no power in this situation. Suddenly, however, the dastardly department of my personality presented two plans, one of which involved dynamite, mustache wax, some rope, and train tracks (all found in aisle seven), which I rejected due to financial investment, and another, much more sinister option, which I accepted.

"Okay," I said with a wide smile. "I'll take two hundred. Thank you very much."

The post office lady got a very satisfied look on her face, cooled her demeanor a bit, and slid the two hundred stamps across the counter as I, in turn, slid her my four dollars. I put my cache in my purse, smiled politely, and walked away. The wheels of the sinister plan moved forward. There was no turning back.

And then I returned the next day.

I boldly stood in line and waited my turn patiently, and when the time had come, I stepped up to the counter and said nicely, "I'd like two hundred two-cent stamps, please."

I could actually see the anger in her face rolling to a boil.

I had her. She had to sell me the stamps. We both knew she had them. She knew I had her.

Her eyes narrowed, and her brow lowered.

"One hundred," she said in a low voice, knowing very well that I did not have her. At all. To the contrary.

Then she pointed her finger at me and said, "Don't you come back. Never come back!"

I was shocked. I couldn't say anything. After closing my mouth, I gathered up my paltry one hundred stamps, turned around, and walked away.

Was I just banned from the post office? I asked myself in disbelief. Did she just ban me from the post office? She just banned me from the post office!

This is ridiculous, I thought, as I stopped myself in the aisle where all the candy that has lost its soul and turned white is kept. How can you ban me from a post office? I'm a *taxpayer*. I'm her boss! And I was going to march right back there and tell her that, but I immediately thought better of making a taxpayer proclamation and pulling a line from the Bill of Rights and distorting it like it was from the Bible or I was Rand Paul. I remembered the numerous times I had passed by this particular drugstore and seen police cars parked outside, making it clear that no one here hesitates to pick up that receiver and call

911. In fact, I think they have someone on the payroll whose job description is solely to "alert the authorities." The store is right next to a bottle-and-can return center, meaning it's a hobo and tweaker destination, full of savory smells and nonsensical muttering, and there's always someone on the pay phone shouting some sort of obscenity to a dealer or a loved one. Not only had I seen cop cars haphazardly parked there, but I'd also had the vast misfortune of being in the drugstore's checkout line when a scuffle erupted from the lotion department. Apparently, according to the person in question, some bath salts had "tumbled into his pocket." The policemen, however, weren't buying it, and instead of cooperating, the accused decided to struggle like he was a wild mustang being lassoed, which is never a good idea in a spot so tiny that bath salts could actually fall into an available opening in your clothing.

As I watched the cops question him, I immediately checked my own coat and pants for tubs of errant body butters.

After the first crash, the man began to scream for help, but I'll be honest and admit I was not about to be the one who volunteered my services. The scuffle moved and ate up more space as the bath-salts plucker thrashed about and screamed louder.

"Call the police!" he demanded. "Somebody call the police!"

"We *are* the police," one of the officers informed him, to which Mr. Salty replied, "I want my *own* police!"

But unfortunately, he was out of luck. Eugene doesn't have that service.

Yet.

Within moments, the altercation had moved in front of the main and only entrance, which I guess was the objective, but it didn't solve any problems for me. It was clear that the situation had the capacity to morph easily from someone who just forgot to take their meds to the headline on the next day's paper that touted a body count. Who knew if Mr. Salty had just come from a knife store, where switchblades may have dropped into his socks, or the bow-and-arrow store, where some may have landed behind his ears; who knew where he had been and what had dropped on him. Bullets. Chain saws. Rope and train tracks. God forbid he had been at the fireworks stand at some point, because any single measure of friction would be enough set that place aglow, and I do not doubt that between the Yankee Candle display and the body-sized sheets of gauze, bottles of gasoline and/or oxygen are fully stocked.

I quickly abandoned my position in line and scurried to the party-plates aisle, in case the thrashing began to spread even farther, because, frankly, I'd rather be crushed by a party-hat tower than gored by a curio or a Department 56 North Pole candy cane.

So, with the memory in my head that when the police cross the store threshold they no longer work for me and the paltry hundred two-cent stamps in my purse, I left the store, mumbling, "Oh yeah? You're not the only post office in town, you know!" and then set out to discover if that was true.

Turns out it was, in fact, true, and I acted smug and felt like I had beaten the Mean Lady at her own game while standing in line at the post office downtown, despite the fact that it had taken me a half hour to snag one of the jumble of metered street spaces. Because this post office doesn't have a parking lot. At all. And because the nineteen people in front of me in line, who had all probably been banned from the satellite station, had gotten there first.

Unlike at the drugstore post office, there is nothing to look at while you wait in line—no fake poo, no pirate condoms, no crime-scene action, nothing to distract you from the other Eugene residents and fellow post-office patrons and their packages. It was then that I saw some amazing things.

For example, I witnessed a lady trying to cram a pound of pistachios *and* a pound of corn nuts into one regular, letter-sized Priority Mail envelope. I couldn't figure out where that lady could possibly be sending corn nuts where there aren't corn nuts ALREADY, unless there was a corn-nut-less province that I was unaware of. And at two pounds in a Priority envelope, it was going to cost her more money to send corn nuts someplace than the corn nuts cost in the first place (unless she was sending them to a prison, but even then, I'll bet corn nuts are a staple in the vending machines). She ripped through three Priority envelopes before the man behind her pointed out that a box would be a better fit and there were several options eight inches away from her right foot at the center counter, which she was leaning on. She tossed the envelope aside and went in for a box, which easily fit her snack foods, but her delight soon turned to unbridled horror when she attempted to close it. Immediately, she began to complain that the box, which was free, courtesy of the post office, was not equipped with "automatic tape," which I think meant "adhesive strip" to those people who don't buy corn nuts by the pound. I then saw two different women with the same unique bear-claw tattoo and a middle-aged woman with bangs cut from the middle of one ear to the middle of the next, who never closed her mouth the entire time she stood in line, which, by the way, was long enough to hatch an egg. From any species.

In addition to the automatic-tape debacle, almost everyone in line had some sort of mail disaster to contend with, whether it was trying to ship vast amounts of liquids and perishable items (how long does it take for a corn nut to perish, anyway? Is it even within the realm of possibilities? I bet corn nuts have been found in the tombs of Egyptian royalty and still taste exactly the same when unearthed), sealing a box up with Scotch tape, or arguing that a customs form was not needed for her package, "because it's just going to *Italy*."*

The next time I had to go to the post office, I went to the branch rumored to have a parking lot, hoping to avoid the downtown contingent and tattoo museum. And I did and was confronted with people who had been unemployed for a long, long time, so long that they had lost perspective of the phrase "time frame" in any conceivable meaning, even though I could easily measure the duration of their life span left on Earth with my fingers. For example, at this post office, I waited in line behind patrons who liked to round out every money-exchanging transaction with a nice, pointless conversation about a) are Disney stamps more expensive than regular stamps; b) what is the difference between a book of stamps and a sheet of stamps; and c) if they write a check, can they write it over the amount and get seven dollars and forty-two cents back?

It was then that I realized it completely wasn't fair for anyone to say ever again that post office employees are slightly askew, because if you were dealing with morons demanding automatic tape for their corn-nut packages day in and day out, things might get a little sketchy for you, too.

I didn't go back to the post office—any of them—for over a year. If I had to mail a package, I'd go to other shipping places that were way more expensive and farther away, and I bought my stamps online. But as I was taping up the box of unders for

---

*The corn-nut lady, by the way, sent her package to some P.O. box in rural Louisiana, where I am positive that not only are corn nuts available, but they're a staple of the diet, along with Karo syrup and obscure pig parts. It's a main protein source. I bet Corn Nut Stew, Corn Nuts and Dumplings, Corn Nut Salad, and Chicken-Fried Corn Nuts are served at every funeral or parole party.

my nephew, I realized that I really didn't want to pay twelve dollars to ship them to Phoenix. Down the street, I could do it for several bucks. It was time, I knew, to try the satellite post office again. Especially if I could save two dollars.

As I stood in line, getting closer to the counter, my heart raced, my mouth got dry, and suddenly I was next.

When she looked up and saw me, she knew. There was no mistaking it. She knew exactly who I was and that I was the Two-Cent-Stamp Bandit. I knew she was the Mean Lady. Her mouth pursed, she looked at me with disdain.

Out of the corner of my eye, I saw something. On her wrist. Bright, colorful, and unmistakably new. An Achilles' heel.

"That," I said, pointing to her hand and the flashy and enormous red, orange, and black outlined dragon on it, "is a lovely tattoo."

Frankly, I have to say that I was shocked. I don't see too many middle-aged Korean post office ladies getting themselves all inked up with medieval symbols and legends, but here we were.

She looked down and knew there was no way out.

She smiled a teeny tiny little bit.

"Thank you," she replied.

"You're welcome," I said. "Those are very pretty colors."

"I think so, too," she added. And looked at the box. "First-class or Priority?"

"Priority," I said. I wanted to show her that I took the post office seriously.

"Any contents that are perishable, liquid, or prohibited?" she asked.

"Nope," I said cheerfully. "Just little-boy's underwear."

Excellent! I realized. By the time I got home, the FBI would be carrying my computer out of the house. But she didn't bat an eye.

"Have a great day!" I said before I left.

We ended that day on decent terms, but when I got home I tracked the package to make sure it had been mailed in the first place, because our trust was new, delicate, and most likely still raw in the middle. I hadn't spent twenty-five minutes looking through irregular underwear in a store that sells matching mommy-and-baby outfits just so the lady at the post office—who I'm sure was certain that I was sending a pound of corn nuts to my husband, who gets very snacky after spending his days working on a Louisiana chain gang—could sit on my package for a week in a slippery act of revenge. Listen. She was a middle-aged Korean woman with a flaming dragon tattoo who'd kicked me out of the post office when I asked for *eight dollars worth of stamps*. In my book, that's a lunatic. Who knew what she was capable of?

But I went back again, and this time I brought two packages. Both Priority. With tracking numbers. I wasn't fooling around.

As she was getting ready to slap the post office label on the second package, someone shouted out to her from the photo department and told her she had a phone call. I watched her face drop as the person informed the Mean Lady that the call was about her daughter.

"Can you wait a minute?" she asked me, her skin tone suddenly ashen.

"Sure," I said.

She went over to the photo department and took the phone call, then returned to the counter a couple of minutes later.

"Thank you," she said. "I was so worried when they said it was about my daughter. But everything's fine; she just wanted to stay at her friend's house longer, so her friend's mom called. I was so scared!"

"I know," I replied. "I saw the look on your face. I'm glad everything is okay."

"Me, too," she said. "Thank you for being so nice about it. You're nice. A lot of people wouldn't have been so nice."

I stopped for a moment.

"I know you must have to put up with a lot working at the post office," I told her, to which she nodded vigorously.

"Some people are crazy," she semi-whispered.

"I know. I've seen it. I saw a lady freak out about *'automatic tape,'*" I informed her, after which I shrugged, furrowed my brow, and mock-laughed loudly.

The Mean Lady nodded. "*I know her!*" she hissed, lightly pounding her fist on the counter.

"And I think you're nice, too," I finished, to which she smiled, nodded, and smoothed the postage label on one of my packages.

"Hey," I said quickly, noticing something very, very odd about her wrist. "Where's your tattoo?"

It was gone. The fiery, tempestuous dragon had vanished.

"Oh," the nice lady said as she laughed and pointed behind her, where on the wall was an entire display of vibrantly colored tattoo decals, including the legendary dragon.

And right then, at that second, we were cooked in the middle.

Butcha Are, Blanche!
Ch'are in That Chair!

❧

Oliver Twist looked at me with more horror in his eyes than I had ever seen on any street urchin, his bowl limply dangling from his hand in shock. Next to him, the Jewish bubbie from Scottsdale was speechless, her missile-sized ta-ta's resting on her belly just above her waist. The Vampire Queen by her side looked on in silence as I lifted my arm up and went in as hard as I could, hitting Jamie, my best friend, in the middle of the back and nearly shooting her out of the wheelchair she was sitting in.

This was not exactly the way I had envisioned my birthday celebration to unfold. I happen to have a Halloween birthday; I am here to tell you that it is not as exciting as it may seem to non-Halloween-birthday people, for the following reasons:

1. There will always be little children interrupting your personal holiday, wanting something from you, and in Oregon you may very well get the gender of the child wrong 100 percent of the time, even when the child in question is wearing a tutu, ballet shoes, and a tiara.
2. There will always be someone you know who is throwing another party on the same night. Sometimes that can get a

little political and can even arrive at a point where people begin Big Talking if they are graduate students, saying things like "But I'm grad-fathered in to throw the Halloweeen party! I've been in grad school longer than anybody else!" when they believe that throwing a birthday party is a call to battle. We discovered that some people with little to focus on tend to lose sight that they're talking about a Halloween party in a crumbling basement apartment that smells like Tinactin and has the filthiest toilet in the county and not something as crucial as Mideast water rights.

And

3. If that trick-or-treat nonsense wasn't enough to cast a pall over my Halloween birthday, I wasn't all that thrilled with rounding my age up yet again, since my age can no longer be mistaken for a football score and has more in common with a high-blood-pressure reading. This was especially true after a well-known person in my town—startlingly close to my age—dropped dead of natural causes and no one seemed particularly shocked but me.

Well, what do you know, I thought, as most people nodded their heads and noted that he would be missed. I was no longer a "tragedy." The rings on this tree were now old growth. In fact, I bet no one would blink an eye if I dropped dead immediately. Instead of muttering "Such a shame, so young" at my funeral, or the preferred "Promising life cut *so short*," people were more apt to whisper something apart from quick, sad clichés. "Well, of course she's dead! Did you see what that girl ate?" would be the more common thing heard at my funeral, followed by "Between you and me, *miracle* she lived to this point. The only regular workout she had involved nothing but her teeth," or "Well, she had a decent run. She lived longer than a caveman," or even "Hey, I just won fifteen dollars! She was top of the list in my Friends and Family Death Pool. Let's celebrate!"

Now continually aware that an ungrievous death was right at my fingertips closest to the saltshaker, I had one hope for my birthday party, and that was simply that I wouldn't be found heaped over the hors d'oeuvres station with guests lifting my limbs and skull for easier access to the onion dip. As long as I survived the celebration, or even if I died and one person cried, I was going to consider it a success.

But so far, everything was going according to plan as the 31st drew nearer. I wasn't hospitalized, needing an organ transplant or atrophying in a coma due to age-related *age*. Instead, I was elated when Jamie mentioned several weeks before that she would drive the hundred miles from Portland to attend, and it was then that I got a brilliant idea. I presented my plan to her and she agreed, saying, "The only thing better than a party is a party where I never have to get up."

And thus it was sealed.

When she arrived at my house on Halloween morning, she had her little suitcase and a satchel with her, and in the suitcase was everything she needed to complete my plan and become her Blanche Hudson to my Baby Jane from the classic camp horror movie.

Jamie and I first watched *What Ever Happened to Baby Jane?* in high school, absolutely glued to the screen as the former vaudeville child star Baby Jane, played by Bette Davis, tormented her sister and former movie star, Blanche, played by Joan Crawford. Ever since then, I had tried to talk Jamie into using the sisters as Halloween characters but had never had much luck. Confined to a wheelchair due to an accident blamed on her drunk and jealous sister, Jane, Blanche—and her pets—are helpless as Jane dives deeper and deeper into boozy rages and insane, delirious tantrums. Honestly, if there's anything more hilarious than an aged drunk with smeared makeup, it's an aged drunk dressed up like a Little Miss pageant contestant reliving her youth in delusions and liquor-fueled hallucinations. True, that's how I plan on spending my retirement, but as soon as you add a witness to a sullied, addled existence, it quickly loses its playful charm. Which sheds some light on why I could never talk a sixteen-year-old Jamie into dressing up on Halloween to flirt with boys at parties in which every single teen male was dressed as Bo or Luke Duke and wanted to spend the end of the night making out with Daisy, not a fifty-year-old malnourished paraplegic.

But now things were different. Although I was still conscious and was not writing letters to everyone I'd ever met asking them to see if they were a kidney match for me, I do have high blood pressure, and my dentist has thrown around the word "implant" like it's a party streamer. Two steps closer to death. I could croak with no warning, and the only tragedy anyone would experience would be showing up on the last day of my estate sale simply to discover that all remaining items had copious amounts of dog hair on them. And at this stage in the game, when my friends "make out" on anything, it means we have a coupon. Clearly, the time was now or never for our activation into the Hudson sisters. Gingerly, I led Jamie/Blanche across the living room to the corner where the wheelchair I had just rented from the medical-supply store awaited her.

"Ooooh," she cooed in a dramatic voice several octaves lower than her own, taking on the patiently proper Blanche persona immediately as she adjusted herself in the chair.

"You didn't eat cha din-din!" I cackled as I channeled Jane, quoting a line from the scene where Jane serves Blanche a feathered friend on a silver plate.

"You wouldn't be able to do these awful things to me if I weren't still in this chair!" Blanche shot back at me accusingly in a dead-on Joan Crawford impression.

"Butcha *are,* Blanche! *Ch'are* in that chair," I replied as I threw my hands up, Bette Davis–style.

It was a stellar performance, and I could already tell it was going to be a night to remember. After we had set the food up and the guests had started to arrive, Jamie parked her wheelchair in the kitchen. She headed toward the breakfast nook, started rifling through her satchel, and then grabbed something.

"What is that?" I asked cautiously.

"Mama's Booze Bag," she said matter-of-factly, and then pulled out a full fifth of Absolut by the neck. She ripped the seal off with her fingernail, using surgical precision, much like a falcon's talon gutting a lemming.

As people began to arrive, it was relatively clear that most of my husband's friends had no idea who Jamie and I were dressed as, and I have to say I wasn't exactly surprised. At a party several years ago, I bought a black shift from Talbots, a Cher-length blond wig, and a plastic baby doll, which I shoved between two pieces of ciabatta bread to make a baby sandwich, and came downstairs as Ann Coulter. I thought it was pure genius and talked loudly over anyone who spoke in my general vicinity, but people spent the evening smiling politely and moving away from me. Not one person cried, "Baby sandwich! Blowhard! Fiend! You're Ann Coulter!" Somehow, everyone ID'd my husband, Hamid Karzai, immediately, even when he was catching non-halal meatballs in his mouth. The only people his costume was lost on were my friends, who had puzzled looks on their faces when they asked me, "I think I get it. . . . Is your husband supposed to be Omar Sharif in *Doctor Zhivago*?"

I was very disappointed about my Ann Coulter costume and searched diligently over the next eleven months for something wicked, funny, and *obvious*. One day it came to me, not in a dream but in a TMZ.com video of Sad Clown Anna Nicole wandering around her backyard, snookered on pharmaceuticals, her face painted like John Wayne Gacy at a kid's party, and mumbling that her belly was upset not because she was pregnant but because she just had to fart. Halfway through the footage, she picked up a plastic baby doll and insisted it was real, and that's when I *knew*. I have that *same baby doll*, I thought. It's the filling in my Ann Coulter sandwich!!

I bought another blond wig, clown makeup, and a sheet to tie around me to duplicate the toga Anna was wearing. I also collected pill bottles and taped Anna's name to them, then Velcroed them to the toga.

Seriously, a *slam dunk*. And then she died. But I was not letting go of my dream and my fantastic costume. In fact, I thought my plaudits to a gassy, wasted Anna Nicole in white, green, and red face were nothing short of a tribute to her greatness.

However, I didn't yet realize that, year after year, I was involved in a tiring game of Stump the English Grad Student, which was remarkably easy to win, unless you had an arcane trivia question about *The Canterbury Tales* or *Daniel Deronda* (that joke is only funny to 0.2 percent of the population, and it's not you); in that case, all hands would pop up and monkey sounds would be made. But anything concerning pop culture and the outside world, forget it. How can this be, I thought as the next person looked at me, my crazy clown makeup *that looked exactly like Anna Nicole's,* and my baby doll, then swiped a carrot through some ranch dip and walked away. I made a mental note to myself that we simply had to start inviting more gay men to our Halloween parties, because they were clearly the only ones with a finger on the pulse of current events.

My husband—that year, Cesar Millan, the Dog Whisperer—wasn't making things any better. Sporting his two-day pencil-thin mustache, he was sitting between a fairy and a girl in a platinum wig who was wearing a tiny tiara and a shiny pink dress that showed altogether too much of her corpulent, goose-pimpled flesh. After standing there for several minutes with absolutely no acknowledgment whatsoever, it dawned on me that not only did the guests not know who I was supposed to be but they didn't know who I *was.* I was completely anonymous and also quite irrelevant.

"Can I get anyone anything?" I said to the crowd, hoping to somehow fit in among the considerable chatter.

"Chhh!" my husband said without looking at me, occupied by other conversation with the gentleman across from him.

"I brought out my laptop," my clown face insisted, nodding to the computer in my hands. "Anybody want to see a video of a Sad Clown Anna Nicole? She says the word 'poot.' "

"Chhh!" my husband said, this time outstretching his arm in my direction without making eye contact.

"Wha—" I began.

"Chhh!" my husband said again, now looking at me and furrowing his brow.

"What are you supposed to be?" I whispered to the girl with the crown of flowers around her head. "Are you the Fairy Queen?"

"I am Peaseblossom, woodland sprite from *A Midsummer Night's Dream,* act three, scene one, line one thousand," she whispered back, and then looked away (again, 0.2 percent. Not you).

"I'm Sad Clown Anna Nicole," I continued in a hushed tone, thinking the sprite was nice.

"Great," she said quickly.

"I bet I know who you're supposed to be!" I said, whispering behind Peaseblossom as I pointed a finger at the girl in the satiny dress. I was about to shout out "Miss Piggy!" when she looked at me, gave me a long, dramatic blink, and said, "I am Marilyn Monroe."

"Wow!" I replied, while inside I reasoned with myself that she *had* been dead for half a century. It might have been an accurate representation for all I knew.

After there had been more drinking involved, it was far easier to force people to watch the Anna Nicole video: I set up a viewing station by the beer cooler and made people say the magic words "Show Me the Sad Clown!" before the cooler lid could be lifted.

But this year I wasn't going to struggle with my costume. I had a great idea—one I had waited half my life to put together—and I was going with it, come hell or high water. Nothing could stop me now. I wasn't worried about the grad students; Jamie and I were a team, and we were sticking together.

After she got the Absolut flowing, Jamie sat in her rolling throne, her hair piled into a spinster's bun, dark circles under her eyes and hollows in her cheeks, her long black gown spread out before her, and a tidy little blue silk scarf tied at her throat, Joan Crawford style.

I was immediately relieved when two of our first guests,

Drew and Jacob—that night visiting our house as Oliver Twist and the Jewish grandma with missile boobs, respectively—walked through the front door and gasped when I wheeled Jamie out.

It was then I knew we had done good. Jamie's makeup was starvation, perfected, and my stage makeup, smeared blood-red lips, and blond pin-curled wig, drunkenly askew, were on the money.

My dream come true.

More and more guests began to arrive, and repeatedly I got a vague smile but no nods of recognition. I barely cared. Jamie and the people who knew that we were the Hudson sisters—including my friend Nancy, who arrived as the Vampire Queen—congregated in the kitchen so Jamie could be closer to her sauce. I walked away for a minute—*a minute, I tell you*—to talk to some friends, and when I came back into the kitchen, Mama's Booze Bag was no longer located in the tote bag: It was sitting in the rolling throne, with a tidy blue scarf tied around its neck.

"How long has she been like this?" I asked Oliver and Maude, who both simply shrugged as Jamie laughed her drunk laugh, which I know by heart. She closes her eyes, throws back her head at the same time she throws up her hands. And she touches people, and Real Life Jamie never does that. I knew that once we passed a certain point of inebriation—to which we were dangerously close—all bets would be off, and our night of fun was either going to end with an unintentional prat-fall or finding her within an hour taking a "nap" on the dog's bed.

"Who knows?" they said together. "Please don't make her stop drinking. She's hilarious!"

"How much did you drink?" I said, grabbing a glass and

filling it up with water. "Do you realize how old we are? We have brittle bones! What if you fell down the stairs? Do you want some water?"

"Sure," she said, as she shrugged and then nodded in a motion that resembled a bobble head. "What's in it?"

"*Water,*" I repeated as I handed it to her. "With a splash of water."

"Oh, good," she said as she reached for the glass. "I would like a little quiche, too, please. With a splash of water. Got that?"

Great, I thought, anything to help soak up the bathtub of vodka that was immersing every cell in her body. I ran and plucked a quiche off the table and handed it to her when she was done laughing. She popped it whole into her mouth, giggled, and then took a drink.

Oh, boy. I knew she had lost any coherency for the night, but maybe if she drank enough fluid to prevent the alcohol from shrinking her brain, she wouldn't lose most of tomorrow dry-heaving and spinning in my guest bedroom, even though "guest bedroom" is a loose term for a blow-up mattress on the floor of my husband's office. I couldn't believe she had gotten drunk without me; she had just taken off like a spooked racehorse, speeding around the track, all by herself! Besides, I had biscuits and gravy planned for the Day After My Birthday Breakfast, and somebody was coming with me even if she had to carry her own retch bucket, though in the past her purse has doubled very effectively for that purpose.

Suddenly I heard a loud gasping sound, and I turned around to see Jamie's sunken-in eyes grow large, then humongous, then exponential.

"What's the matter?" I cried, although the only response she gave me was another desperate long gasp.

The quiche! I thought. It's lodged in her throat! Holy shit, she's choking. *She's choking.*

Jamie's hands flew up around her neck. She tried to draw another breath in.

Her face was turning red.

There was no time to waste. No one, no matter what their age or how likely it was that they didn't exercise or have an age-appropriate heart rate, was going to die on my watch.

Not at my party!

I immediately shifted into *Laurie: Panic Level One: Strike Offense!* © 2011, during which my first impulse is typically always blunt-force trauma.

"I'm going to hit you!" I warned, and she nodded frantically, still terribly, horribly silent.

I pushed her forward with one hand and brought my other hand behind me. Then I struck her. Square in the back, right between her shoulder blades.

Oliver Twist, Maude Greenberg, and Nancy, the Vampire Queen, stood and watched as Baby Jane Hudson beat the living shit out of Blanche.

Nobody said a word.

Whack. Whack. Whack.

I hit her several times, but I couldn't dislodge the quiche chunk. Precious seconds were ticking away as smaller and smaller amounts of oxygen were getting to my best friend's brain, although I have to admit that, with the amount of vodka she had just poured down her throat, there probably wasn't much of a difference from ten minutes prior.

All I knew was that I wasn't saving her, her eyes were beginning to bulge, and, before I knew it, I had arrived at *Laurie: Panic Level Two: TV Moves!* © 2011.

So I guess it is necessary to mention here that if you reach a level of danger—life-threatening or otherwise—in my presence, I will most likely lunge at you like I did to Jamie and lock my arms under your breasts.* In other words, I will Heimlich you.

Admittedly, I don't have much experience with this sort of technique and I never took a class, but I did it once to my dog and she stopped coughing, so I tend to think my success rate is pretty good. Or at least better than most. But at this juncture, I didn't think I had any choice. Jamie was choking, her face was an even deeper red, I had exhausted all of the tools at my disposal. I had nothing left.

I went in.

In fact, it probably didn't resemble the Heimlich maneuver as much as it did me trying to wrestle a corpse out of the ocean, but I wasn't doing it for the glamour. Heimliching people is not as easy as it appears on TV, especially if you're behind the victim, who is in a wheelchair that keeps rolling away across the kitchen, and you have to keep Heimliching her as you move to other rooms of the house.

Still, no one said anything, and although I didn't notice it at the time, in hindsight I'm not sure if it was because the bystanders were speechless at activities at my party or because

---

*Disclaimer: I can't say for sure if I touched Jamie's boobs or not. I think it is altogether possible though unlikely, due to the fact that I pride myself on having a built-in, natural "hot stove" mechanism to avoid that sort of thing and have been 100 percent successful in the past concerning such. In the case that there was a videotape of the whole event, however, and it was played for a jury during an assault trial or something along those lines, it might document the fact that I did, indeed, encounter her boobs in one manner or another. And I am sorry for that if my built-in mechanism of best-friend boob avoidance did not activate. But there was a flurry of activity exploding around me, not to mention the fireworks of survival egging me on, so I suppose the natural mechanism could have been overwritten and catastrophe experienced. Therefore, you should expect that if the Panic Level reaches Level Two, a side breast or under area might be unintentionally grazed. It is within the possibilities of natural movement and lifesaving, and it is both necessary and essential not to read between the lines.

the heroine was wearing a faceful of smeared Joker pancake makeup and had a ratty pin-curl wig tacked to her head.

And you know, the next thing I learned was that the last thing you kind of want to do after someone has consumed a liter of vodka and a host of little quiches is to toss them around like a baby you are angry at. Suddenly, Jamie covered her mouth. Which was, technically speaking, a sign of life (*Laurie: Panic Level Two: TV Moves!* © 2011—two for two!) but also a sign of something much more sinister.

"No!" I screamed. "Oh, no! You cannot throw up in the wheelchair! I don't wanna buy a wheelchair! Please don't make me buy a wheelchair!"

Now, I know it sounds cruel to yell at someone I had been trying to yank from the claws of death only moments before, but I had to give the medical-supply place my credit card! I had to fill out a two-page questionnaire about who was going to use the wheelchair, where we were going with it, and who the primary caretaker of the wheelchair was going to be. I had to have the skill of a surgeon to evade their questions so they wouldn't figure out I simply needed it as a prop for a costume. If it came back scuffed or scratched, that was one thing—old people fall out of stuff all the time—but if I brought this thing back with eau de Mama's Booze Bag with a note of bile, I had just purchased a new mode of transportation.

"How is this a surprise to anybody?" people would now say at my funeral. "One day, she's walking; the next day, she won't go anywhere without the wheelchair. She just gave up."

Suddenly, a little choking person I know popped up out of the wheelchair and ran to the bathroom, where she stayed for a long, long, long time, and when she came out, she was no longer the jolly drunk who had been stationed in the kitchen.

"Are you all right?" I asked as she looked at me, clearly irritated. "I can't believe a mini-quiche almost killed you."

Jamie shook her head, her eyes red and watery. "It wasn't the quiche," she slurred. "The water went down the wrong pipe. I just needed a minute to clear my throat, but I was stuck in that stupid thing. I couldn't get away from you. You wouldn't have been able to keep shaking me if I wasn't in that chair."

"But you *were* in that chair," I said quietly, not able to look at her. "You *were*."

Then she went off to bed, a full night's excitement over by 9:15 P.M.

When I woke up the next morning, Jamie was already downstairs, miraculously, drinking coffee with my husband.

"Whatever happened last night, I'm sorry," she began.

"You don't remember?" I asked quickly.

"Not very much," she admitted. "It's all sort of a blur. A crazy black blur. Did we get on a trampoline?"

"She Heimliched you!" my husband cried immediately, pointing at me. "While she was wearing her crazy Baby Jane Hudson outfit!"

Jamie looked puzzled. "Why did you do that?" she asked.

"I thought you were choking on a mini-quiche," I explained. "So I tried to save you. Your eyes were all bulgy, you were turning red, it was terrifying. But look! You're alive!"

She shook her head. "Yeah, I guess," she replied. "I don't remember any of that. That must have been the part where I thought we were jumping. So that explains the smell and the taste in my mouth."

"Yep," I said, nodding.

"But I can't move my arm," she continued. "My back is

killing me. What did I do that I can't move my arm? Or basically any of my torso?"

I just shook my head and thanked God I'd hit her in a place where she couldn't see the bruise.

"No idea, but I'm starving!" I exclaimed. "Let's go for biscuits and gravy. And make sure you grab your purse."

You Must Be My Lucky Star

❦

"You need to stop eating in bed," my husband said, after I had just gotten all comfy under the covers. "I know you're eating candy in here. Please don't do it again."

"I don't eat candy in bed," I protested, surprised that he would even think such a thing.

"But you do," he said, laughing at me. "Look at my pillow. It's covered in melty bits of chocolate that fell out of your mouth during one of your nighttime Ambien candy binges. All I'm asking is that you eat the candy downstairs and don't bring it in here."

I looked at his pillow and, sure enough, it had dots of what looked like little chocolate stars on one side of it.

"Well, that's not me," I argued. "I have nothing to do with that."

"Well, I don't know what else it could be," he mentioned one last time, and turned out the light.

I didn't know what it could be, either, I thought. I really wasn't eating candy in bed. That I remembered, anyway. That was ridiculous. Wouldn't I remember eating candy in bed, even if Ambien Laurie had participated in a nighttime chocolate binge? There would be evidence, I reasoned. She's a pig. She leaves wrappers everywhere. Or little bites of things. Or it would still be in my hair. It was impossible, I reasoned, because otherwise it would be too sad to be true. One should always remember eating chocolate.

So the next morning I searched the house for empty Hershey's wrappers or anything comparable that Ambien Laurie might have attacked. I suddenly remembered I had a bar of dark chocolate to make frosting saved in the spice cabinet, and I started feeling very, very guilty that I was the Chocolate-Star Bandit. But then I opened the cabinet door and it was still there, nestled in its as-yet-untouched wrapper.

I didn't find anything, and I knew that if I didn't find it, she didn't eat it.

Two nights later as I climbed into bed, however, my husband had his pillow in his hands and was closely examining it. Then he looked at me with his lips pursed.

"I don't know if you think this is funny," he told me. "But I already asked you to stop eating candy in bed. Now it looks like this is one big joke to you. There are more chocolate stars on my pillow."

I threw my hands up and shrugged.

"You got me," I said honestly. "There's not even any chocolate in the house besides Baker's chocolate. I looked all over yesterday morning, and nothing. I don't know what you want me to say. All I can tell you is that it's not me."

"*Very funny*. I hope you're getting a big laugh out of this," he said as he turned over, rammed his head into the chocolate-star pillow, and turned out the light.

Whatever, I thought. I didn't know what to say. What was I supposed to do, confess to something that I knew I hadn't done, just to make my husband think that I wasn't playing a joke on him? Plus, this wasn't the first time that my husband had misidentified something.

When he was a kid, it was his job to take out the trash, and inevitably, because he was seven, the trash sometimes piled up. When his mother would take him to task and make him do his job, garbage would end up getting spilled on the way out to the alley, because there was so much of it. It was during one of those unfortunate runs that my husband discovered that trash—once an unenviable chore that he hated—was actually a treasure trove of toys. He looked at the bounty spread out before him on the sidewalk; there were cardboard rolls, tinfoil balls that could be made into anything, and little white telescopes. Tons of them. So many of them that he couldn't figure out how these marvelous things had not been seen before. Obviously, they had come from the house, and someone was throwing these perfectly good tiny telescopes away! The fools he lived with! Idiots! Why were they keeping these from him? He surveyed the land through them, pretended to be a pirate, and gathered them together to add to the telescope collection that he kept in a shoe box in his room. He even found special pink plastic ones, which he considered far more collectible and rarer than the regular white ones.

Now, I'm not sure when he discovered that he most likely had one of the world's only collections of Tampax applicators under his bed in a shoe box, or that he realized he had been mashing them up to his face, but it just goes to show that sometimes what you think is a magical gift from the toy gods is really a confusing nightmare that you'll only reveal when you've been drinking heavily at parties. And I have to say that, honestly, many, many years later (although the wounds still heal), his method of discovery has not exactly changed. Or improved.

Yesterday, someone I live with pulled a jar of salsa out of the fridge, opened it, and said, "There's white all in there. What do you think that is?"

I said I didn't know and told him to taste it, but the person put the lid back on the jar and returned it to the fridge. After a second, I asked him why he put it back and he said, "You might eat it."

So clearly we're still facing challenges in the mystery-solving department, and if my husband happened to touch his pillow with muddy fingers and forgot about it, that really wasn't my fault. Or my problem.

But the next day I was bringing some laundry up to the bedroom when I saw my little geriatric cat, Barnaby, walking along the bed near the headboard. Honestly, I didn't like the cat walking all over my bed, but he was old and I doubted he was going to see another ring grow under his bark, if you know what I'm saying. I thought, fine, walk on the bed. I love pulling animal fur out of my mouth at three in the morning.

He was flitting around on the bed, and when I went to put some of my husband's socks away, he came to that side of the bed and promptly sat down on my husband's pillow, square in the center.

"Oh, you need to get off that," I said, and lifted him up, repositioning him on the comforter pointing toward my side. He was happy. His little stump of a tail was up and he flicked it.

I gasped.

"I know that star!" I said as I snapped my fingers in victory. *"I knew I wasn't eating candy!"*

That night, my husband got into bed with a book in his hand, ready to have a nice, relaxing bedtime, but then he noticed a new chocolate star right smack in the center of the pillow.

He looked at me and shook his head.

"I don't know how or why this is hilarious to you, but it is annoying to me," he informed me, and he put the pillow behind him.

"I told you I have nothing to do with that," I replied.

I grabbed Barnaby from the edge of the bed and turned his tail toward my husband.

"But does *this* look familiar?" I asked.

He looked at Barnaby, then the pillow, then Barnaby, then the pillow, and I almost thought he was going to reach for the cat and put it back in the fridge in case I might still eat it.

"Let me give you a hint: I wouldn't wish on this one!" I said.

My husband shook his head. "I just don't know where you're going with this," he said, getting a wee bit angry. I knew I had to cut to the chase.

"May I present," I said, doing some fancy game-show-hostess finger moves under my cat's ass, "Barnaby's Little Chocolate Star!"

Then I moved his tail down like a lever. "IT'S AN ASS," I said with the tail down.

"It's a stamp!" I said, lifting the tail up.

"It's an ass," I said, moving the tail back down again.

"It's a sta—"

My husband looked me dead in the eye.

"You need to tell me right now that you've been eating chocolate in this bed," he said firmly.

And, in a way, I wished I could have. But I already knew what movie was playing in my husband's head, and it was of him, fast asleep and drooling all over the chocolate stars, then, in slow motion, rubbing and nuzzling his face all over it. And my version is the same, but he is even smiling, which I know he is not doing in his, and mine rounds out nicely with a laugh track behind it, too.

Because it was true, and I knew it was true. He could have buffed that pillow to a shine with all the rubbing he'd been doing against that thing. I offered to have a lineup so my husband could identify the right butt, but he quickly declined.

"Oh, honey," I said reaching out comfortingly. "I'm sorry that I didn't lie to you and that I repeatedly told you the truth, and that for the past four nights you've been sleeping on a pillow that your cat shit-stamped on both sides with his leaking asshole. Maybe now you should change your pillowcase."

"Shut up," my husband said, as he shot off the bed and stomped down the hall and stairs to the linen closet. "I'm probably going to have cholera!"

"That's good," I yelled back. "Because it's still in the jar in the fridge."

Instant Karma

M y dentist looked at the X-ray and then looked back at me.

"How'd you do it this time?" he asked.

"Trying to teach a hippie a lesson at Trader Joe's," I answered.

"Well, not only is that a waste of your time," he replied, "but it's going to cost you twelve hundred dollars."

I nodded in agreement and rolled my eyes. Sure, I should have known better, but sometimes the moment arrives when you do or die; either you take a stand or you shrink away and shut up forever.

When we first moved to Eugene, I understood that it was my duty to adapt to my new environment instead of expecting my new environment to adapt to me. But that proved far more difficult than originally expected, because, you see, we moved to a place that is the homeland to the horror of FaerieWorlds. It's an annual Eugene festival in which anyone can spend twenty dollars a day to wander in and out of crafts booths staffed by people who decided they could make a better living weaving fairy crowns out of polyester ribbons and dead grass than investing in a couple of semesters in community college.

Pan is hanging out on every corner, the prosthetic-elfin-ears vendor sells out, and no one there has ever heard of hair conditioner. It's similar to a Renaissance Fair but with more demons and flutes. (And if you can even explain the difference to me, you win. I happen to think the two are rather synonymous.)

However, that's not to say this is Eugene on a daily basis but rather to show what the petri dish that could birth something of the magnitude of FaerieWorlds looks like. The challenge I was up against was somewhat larger than initially estimated, but I convinced myself I could do it.

While Phoenix certainly isn't a bastion of normalcy—you can take your gun anywhere you can take a baby, and that's the law—it seemed far easier to make friends there. I found it difficult to fit in when we arrived in Eugene but naturally thought it would pass and that I would eventually find my people. They had to be out there somewhere, right? I clearly recall the exact moment I realized how much trouble I was in and when I first felt hope flush away. My husband was also trying to make new friends and had invited a cohort from grad school and Shakespeare scholar, Bennet, to a baseball game at the historic WPA stadium down the street from our house. I was on the phone with my sister when Bennet arrived, and when my husband announced that they were going to go, I hung up the phone to meet my husband's new pal. He was very nice, very polite, on the reserved side, but that's fine, I was meeting him for the first time. Shy is fine. His name is Bennet and he studies Shakespeare, I reminded myself. So I decided to break the ice a little bit by relating a story that my sister had just told me on the phone.

It seemed that her son Nicholas, who at the time was about nine, had just gotten into honors math, which was exciting because now someone in our family besides my father could do fractions, and having an understudy would come in very handy when cutting birthday cake. She told me that he had also joined band and had taken up the clarinet, which we were less excited about. Not that playing a clarinet is a bad thing, but in a year, when the kid got braces, if he was walking down the street wearing a Mathletes shirt and carrying a clarinet, even *I* would have to beat him up.

Apparently, however, Nicholas, who is a perfectionist, was a little upset that his mother only rented the instrument and didn't buy it. But clarinets ran about $450, so to buy something we were hoping he'd suck at was out of the question.

"At least he hadn't figured out yet that a shitload of other kids already had their mouths all over it before he did," I relayed as I started laughing. "My sister said he's trying so hard to play it right, but he's shoving the damned mouthpiece in so far he's making himself gag on it."

I thought at least my husband would laugh, but, instead, the two of them stood there smiling very nicely, which wasn't the response I expected at all. I mean, my nephew is gagging himself on a member of the woodwinds family, and *that is hilarious*. I decided I must not be explaining it very well, so I added, "Not a good look for fifth grade."

Again, nothing but stiff smiles, and I didn't get it. It was a funny story; what was missing, what hadn't I said?

Then I did the unthinkable, just to make sure I drove that punch line home, deep, deep, deep into the ground so no one could miss it: I very quickly, although apparently quite accurately, imitated a little boy gagging on a clarinet.

And I wasn't even done with my imitation, I was still in the middle of it when I realized that I was doing something highly regrettable, and my mouthful of pretend clarinet sort of melted away with any chance of humor the story might have had.

When I looked at my husband, his lips were tight across his face in a frown, and he said simply, "Wow, that's quite a story, Laurie. Are you ready, Bennet?"

I was pretty sure that, in one swipe of unintentional pornographic charades, I had ruined everything. My first introduction to one of my husband's colleagues and that's what I did. I mean, tell that story to an undergrad, sure, no problem, but to a nineteenth grader, a Shakespeare scholar no less? I once fell asleep at a performance of *Macbeth* I was so bored, and I was playing one of the witches. All I could do was hope that my husband and Bennet got seats behind home plate and that some freak fly ball would boomerang and bounce off Bennet's head, creating no physical marks or lasting effects but memory loss from an hour prior to the game.

At least I was on my own when I destroyed the dreams of innocent children of Eugene during a potluck at my neighbor's house last summer. I mean, if you were invited to a gathering and it was going to be full of kids, what would you bring? You would bring cupcakes, right? Homemade, straight-from-the-box cupcakes with thick, swirly chocolate frosting and sprinkles on them. Right? Isn't that what you would bring?

So that's how I arrived, with a tray full of cupcakes that I spent the morning making and decorating, thirty cupcakes in all, which, honestly, I felt wouldn't be enough. I was already down for three of them, so that left twenty-seven for everyone else, and if there were even ten kids there at three apiece, supply was short.

I placed them on the table, carefully took the tinfoil off, and exposed the bounty of the little round cakes of heaven below. And the children gathered, glowing at the sight of the shiny frosting and the happy rainbow sprinkles. They crowded all around the tray, each deciding on which was going to be theirs.

One girl, who looked to be about eight, was the first to reach her hand out, her middle finger and thumb making the spread in preparation for a landing, when she looked at me and said:

"Are these vegan?"

Thank Cheezus I wasn't drinking anything, because my mouth would have rained over the entire tray.

Instead, I laughed. "Goodness, no!" I said in my Nice Neighbor Lady Who Makes Cupcakes voice. "Those are *real* cupcakes, right out of the Betty Crocker box, I can assure you!"

And just like that, the little girl retracted her formerly happy hand, the glee on her face turned forlorn, her head dropped, and she simply said, "Oh."

Her mother came forward and patted her on the back and said to me, "She's vegan. She made that choice when she was three."

It was quite possibly the saddest thing I had ever heard. That child, apparently, had never had a Pop-Tart. Cocoa Puffs. Fritos!

Then the mom said to the tiny vegan, "I'm sorry that they aren't the right kind."

Immediately, all of the other little children backed away from the tray as if someone had said they were poocakes.

Now, I'm sure you are thinking, were they really children, or were they adults who hadn't eaten protein or calcium in so many years that their bone structure was actually in an advanced state of atrophy and they appeared much smaller than people who eat *food*? Because that's sort of what I was inclined to believe, and, I'm sorry, but when I was three, *cotechinata*— pork skin rolled up with garlic, parsley, and parmesan cheese, then cooked in tomato sauce—was my favorite food. My mother simply called it "skin." When I asked her what the "skin" on my plate was, she looked at me and said, *"Skin,"* and when it was apparent I wasn't getting it, she pointed to her arm and said, *"Skin,"* again, as in, "Skin is skin, what don't you get?" Now, I don't know what that lady was feeding her vegan kid for her to make that choice, but it took me years to finally understand what my mother was talking about. And then, sure, yeah, I quit asking for "skin." Didn't quit asking for bacon or ham sandwiches, but at three I certainly didn't equate something as blatant as the skin on my mother's arm with my favorite food. I'm not saying that the story about the three-year-old vegan isn't true, just that if someone had eaten a real, moist, spongy cupcake with buttercream frosting piled on top prior to making a declaration that would ruin a Nice Neighbor Lady's potluck experience five years later, the outcome that day might have been different. All I'm saying is that maybe she didn't have all the information at hand when she made a definitive decision about a minuscule bit of butter and an egg. That's what I'm saying. And for the record, upon hearing that I had decided to become a vegan at three, my mother would have shook her head as she informed me, "Well, either you should find another family or you're going to be hungry a lot, little girl, because I'm frying an animal right now."

My neighbor—the hostess—and her daughter both noticed what was going on at the cupcake portion of the table and immediately came over and grabbed cupcakes for themselves, and I will forever love them both for it. But when I left a while later, twenty-five cupcakes, more or less, still sat on the tray, refused and rejected like little girls whose thighs touched and who couldn't run to too many bases before asking to go to the nurse after the teams were picked for softball.

I still insist my cupcakes are the right kind. It's cupcakes without eggs and butter that are weird. And at the next potluck we were invited to later that summer, I brought napkins. Someone else, as you might have guessed, brought cupcakes. Made from gluten-free flour and a wish, was my estimation. I had a Revenge Cupcake, just to be polite, just to take the high road, and I can report that it was nothing conversion-worthy. Chances are you'll see me strutting a burqa before you'll see me stop loading a heap of bacon in my mouth. But if I thought the cupcake disaster was a true Eugene experience, there was nothing that could prepare me for what happened several weeks later.

It was a lovely evening, a gathering of grad students and their spouses, significant others, and partners (you have to say all three). The sun was letting go of the brightest part of the day and people were chatting and having conversation when I looked up and saw a young woman several feet away ease the strap of her top down—like she was in a dirty dressing room at Ross—pull her arm through it, and then bring her boob out. Uncovered. Exposed. Unabashed. Then it flopped like a fish and hung loosely, like it had a hook through it, while she had a conversation with two other people. There it remained, exposed to the elements and accessible to anyone who needed to wipe their hands.

I don't know where the baby was. It wasn't on her, *that's* for sure. I don't know if the baby ever came in for a landing or what. The baby was not in the general vicinity when the incident began. Maybe the baby had a GPS device implanted and this was all prep work, but I think it would have been more considerate if she had a visual of the baby before I had a visual of her. And the boob sat there, and sat there, and sat there. It actually behaved very quietly for the ten minutes it was left to roam free in my field of vision before I could talk to someone else and face a different direction.

I had never been at a barbecue before in which one person was playing a solo version of spin the bottle without notifying anyone else. Frankly, I didn't know how to react, so I didn't. I just attempted to carry on with my conversation, though every thirty seconds or so my eyes would shoot over to see if the boob had made a retreat. It had not. Honestly, I thought I had to be seeing things, as in "I had a feeling I put too much salt on the potato salad and now I am having a stroke and experiencing horrifying hallucinations of hippie breasts," and then I convinced myself that I simply must have gotten two pills confused an hour earlier and ended up taking a whole Ambien instead of a Beano.

And you know, I really have to say this: If your baby isn't even in the room and you can't bear to come equipped with a blanket, kindly put your boob away in its rightful compartment. Don't leave it hanging out for ten to fifteen minutes at a barbecue like you're waiting for someone to hang a Christmas ornament on it. In hindsight, maybe what I should have done was run over to stand next to her, whip out my own bewbie, and cry, "Oh! I didn't know there was a contest! Look, I win! My boob still looks like a boob, since I can't fold it in half like a taco."

Now, I know that babies get hungry and babies need to be fed, but this wasn't about breast-feeding, because there was no feeding going on for the portion of an hour that the teat got a tan. This was about pulling a private part of your body that resembles a tortilla with an eraser located randomly at the bottom edge of it out at a party and letting it sit there because you don't know the meaning of the word "inappropriate."

But apparently I was the odd one out here, because when I mentioned this to a group of people several weeks later, someone asked me if I was ashamed of my own body, which, honestly, didn't have anything to do with the topic of a free-range boob at a social gathering. I wasn't the one softly cajoling the boob out from under its tank top. And frankly, the answer to that question is that I am downright proud of my boobs; I had the best boobs at that party, because I have more faith in my bra than I have in my accountant, and you'd have a better chance selling someone a meat grinder in this town than you would anything with a Maidenform tag on it. There are hippie boobs everywhere, and if you like 'em lean, long, swingy, and Stretch Armstrong-y, this is your boob command center. I, on the other hand, have been devout every day since my charges popped on the scene when I was ten, and they have served me well ever since. I have a huge ass and I have a blap (hybrid of a belly + a lap), but you reap what you sow, and I have plowed a lifetime of underwire fields. Believe me, if there was anyone who deserved to be showing off that day, it was me. Instead, it was the shocking horror of that boob that made a cameo, and, to put it bluntly, in a lineup I would have definitely identified it as a Kombai of Papua New Guinea, considering that it looked like a rooty yam.

So things, all in all, weren't working out that well for me in Eugene. I had offended, shocked, and disgusted large portions of the population, including intelligent people, children with morals, and anyone with offspring, and I was quickly on my way to being on the shit list of the police when I picked up the phone one night at 10:20 P.M. because a cover band at a house party down the street had been blasting all night and was now halfway through another excessively loud, terrible song.

"This is ridiculous," I told the operator as soon as she answered the phone. "This band is so loud! Right now they're playing Loverboy's 'Turn Me Loose'! Who wants to *hear* that? Who wants to *play* that?"

"Loverboy does, ma'am," she told me. "They're at the county fair. Noise ordinance goes into effect at ten-thirty. Is ten minutes too long for you to hang on? They'll probably play 'Working for the Weekend' next."

I said thank you and shut up; I know when to take my hits. Then I ran upstairs, where my husband was getting ready for bed, and shrieked, "Oh my God! Loverboy is at the fair! The police said they're going to play 'Working for the Weekend' next! It's Loverboy! It's *Loverboy*!"

After the incident with the Eugene Police Department put me in my place, I tried to keep a low profile, even when I was putting groceries into my car at Safeway and a guy with a black goatee, long black hair in a tight ponytail, sharp widow's peak, and black pigeon eyes who was parked across from me walked up to his car—a black shiny Mustang with a full-sized skull on the dashboard. He clicked his car alarm, it revved the engine with no one in it, and then I saw the license plate: DIABLO. I assumed that even Hell needs milk and spray pancakes.

I kept quiet when I was at Kinko's and saw the Angel of Death walk in—who, by the way, is a three-hundred-pound teenager with face paint and tiny pigtails, wearing black feathered wings as wide as a Mini Cooper, and who pulled out a frilly parasol while waiting for the bus. And yes, she smoked. Just in case there was a question.

And when I saw a "free box" on a corner, I said, "Guess what, Eugene hippies? When you start a 'free pile' on the corner, you're not recycling; you're just throwing your old filthy shit on a corner. Because no one wants your punctured football, your camping chair missing an arm, the tube from your bong, or anything that touched your body. Really. *Nobody*," but only to myself.

But then wonderful things started to happen that seemed

rather indigenous. It was the first gorgeous day with sun after a very long, rainy winter. My husband and I went down and had garden burgers at a restaurant by the river, sat outside, and watched two people behind us drink several pitchers of beer, then totally break up, complete with lots of crying from both parties.

As soon as they left, the lady sitting behind me informed her dinner companions that "I can't have a library card, because felons can't have library cards. I'm learning a lot about this felon thing." This was almost better than what I'd overheard a waitress say when someone asked her what she was doing over spring break and her response was, "I'm going to California to turn myself in."

And one day, when the weather had turned back to rain, I was waiting to make a left-hand turn when a woman in a Rascal entered the crosswalk. In Eugene, you are not allowed to make any progress on your turn until the person in the crosswalk is safely on the sidewalk on the other side of the street, so I knew I was in for a wait. As I sat there, she rolled along slowly, an enormous Raisa Gorbachev fur hat resting atop her head and a full-length yellow rain poncho draped around her, making her look like a Dole banana float. She was wearing blue hospital socks, and I know what they are because I have a pair just like them. Then the wind kicked up turbulently, and her poncho fluttered at the edges and was picked up by a gust of wind that flipped it over her head, completely blinding her.

But she made no attempt at all to pull the poncho away as she veered off course and into the intersection and slowly, at two to three miles an hour, headed right toward my car. I could only cover my gaping mouth as I watched her get closer and closer, the hum of her scooter getting gradually louder and louder. I had no idea what to do. I couldn't go anywhere, according to Eugene law; I had to stay exactly put until she got onto the sidewalk. Still, she advanced, believing that she would roll up onto the other side at any moment now but instead aiming right into the center of the intersection. So I did the only thing I could do, which was roll down the window and scream, "Hey! Big Banana! You're going the wrong way!" But she apparently didn't hear a word over the wind and just kept humming toward me.

All right, I told myself. Brace for it. Accept it. She's going to hit your car, she's going to scratch the paint with her stupid basket, and then the rest of Eugene can hate you, too. But when she got within ten feet of my car, another miracle blast of wind came up on the other side and flopped the yellow poncho right back to where it was supposed to be. The Big Banana and I locked eyes, our destinies so close to being intertwined.

"You're going the wrong way," I shouted to her again, and pointed to the sidewalk. "You need to be over there."

Without a moment's hesitation, she looked at me, said simply, "You shouldn't hate old people," then put it in reverse, and, although it took her an additional light to make it back up onto the sidewalk, I finally got to turn left.

So things were starting to look up, I thought. There's a lot of fun to be had here. It wasn't as if I hated Eugene; quite the contrary. I really loved it. The landscape was unparalleled, the general citizenry was incredibly nice, people you've never seen before always greeted you with a smile or hello when passing on the street, and I had an adventure near every single time I left the house. In Eugene, there was excitement, beauty, and friendly people. You really couldn't ask for anything more of a town. Maybe things aren't so bad, I realized; it might just take me awhile to find my spot here, that's all. I was sure that I could make my peace with Eugene and that Eugene could make its peace with me. I just needed to be on the lookout for breast-feeding flash mobs and bring nothing but napkins to potlucks. I was positive, after all, that once I had seen a hundred boobs at a barbecue, the horror would eventually erode, like the cliffs of Dover. I realized that everything was going to be all right.

Until I was at Trader Joe's one day, where I noticed there was a table set up near the coffee station that was giving out free samples of something in little paper cups. But the process of sampling wasn't working out as well as it could have, mainly because as soon as the sample girl put a cup out, a bearded old-man hippie, who had strategically stationed himself between the dairy section and the coffee counter, would take a step, swipe the sample, and toss it back like it was a tequila shot before anyone else had a chance to get near it.

I couldn't believe it. I stood down at and watched him as he swiped seven in a row, taking some of them directly from beneath the fingertips of other shoppers trying to get a sample. His stealth was amazing, I will admit, but it was getting out of hand. But this is a thing in parts of this enclave: Free samples are just an open invitation for someone to park themselves and feed for the afternoon. I firmly believe that Eugene was founded when one person with ill-placed intentions left a bowl of spelt crackers out in the middle of the forest with the sign FREE on it; the hippies descended upon it like ants and then stayed, waiting around, playing drums, and popping their boobs out until the next free sample bowl was produced. I've seen a line of twenty-five people crowd together for the opportunity to eat one free raspberry at the farmers' market. ONE FREE RASPBERRY. I mean, really. It's only a free raspberry. For two bucks, you can buy a whole carton, and there's nobody in *that* line.

Watching the sample swiper, I felt my anger rise quickly, and as I saw the sample girl getting ready to put another specimen out, I left my cart, marched over to the table, and literally stole the sample right out from underneath him. "That's what you get for being rude" was the message, and I believe it was successfully parlayed in my evil grin as I walked away with the sample in hand. My success, however, was quickly dampened when I looked down and saw what the sample was: peach salsa and a tortilla chip. No wonder they were giving it away, I thought. It looked disgusting. But just in case the hippie was looking at me, I took the tortilla chip, scooped up the salsa, then threw the cup away in the trash, and on the first bite felt a shot of pain up the left side of my face.

A week later, I was in the dentist's chair after I got the X-rays taken, and my dentist was shaking his head.

"You didn't even want the salsa but you ate it anyway?" he said to me, chuckling.

"He was being rude," I insisted. "And I decided to teach him a lesson."

"What was the lesson?" he asked, still laughing.

"Instant karma's gonna get you," I replied.

"And, oh, did it," he replied. "Because I'm afraid I don't give out free samples."

"Ask Your Grandmother
What a Hairy Tongue Is"

❦

Sitting in the waiting room at my doctor's office, I looked next to me and glared at my husband. When we arrived, he had almost any seat in the house to choose from while I checked in, and when I was done forking over my insurance info I joined him across from the only other lady in the waiting area. Fifteen seconds after I sat down, she burst forth with a rattle that sounded more like a machine gun submerged in Jell-O than the recognizable cough of a mammal.

Before I could even say something like "We need to build a barrier out of magazines and Fisher-Price toys," a grown man walked by in his pajamas, and the sounds of another violently retching in a nearby bathroom were more than audible.

Before the nurse called my name, a man in the third scooter I had seen in ten minutes shot by with a gallon bag full of urine hanging off his front basket on what appeared to be a pee hook.

"Really?" I asked my husband when I regained the ability to speak and say mean things. "Really? Do you know how long it takes to pee a gallon? At least a couple of days. At least. *Days*. And you can't tell me Mr. Rascal hasn't passed a sink since Monday."

My husband just looked at me.

"That," I said as I pointed down the hall in the direction he rolled, "was for shock value. One wrong pass by a magazine rack or sudden jolt over a broom handle and that thing will rupture and have no mercy within a ten-foot splash zone. What would you do if you got soaked by week-old pee and you saw the guy it came from? *Fire*. Fire is the only answer. I'm going to have nightmares for three nights about that humming urinal on wheels. This is why I hate coming here. I don't know why I let you talk me into this."

"You got stabbed in the foot by a pair of scissors," my husband replied. "And you're here because you haven't had a tetanus shot in twenty years, although I do agree that if lockjaw can also paralyze your tongue into silence, I will take you home right now."

That is roughly why I was there. The day before, I had been looking for a specific pair of shoes in my closet and was pulling down a shoe box from a shelf when I saw something flash by and hit my foot, then felt a twinge of pain. But honestly, I didn't think it hurt all that much, until I looked at it and saw blood pumping out of it as if Jed Clampett had been shooting at some food.

I was already standing in a puddle of blood that was spreading quickly, but after I hobbled downstairs and got the bleeding to stop, I realized the wound was deeper than it was wide.

"Oooh, you're going to need a tetanus shot for that," my husband said, wincing.

"Shut up," I replied quickly. "No. I can weather this. Prairie medicine."

My husband rolled his eyes.

"Break your toe, break your nose, fine, go ahead with the prairie medicine," he said. "But lockjaw is a different story.

That will make your body flip around like a little girl possessed by the devil doing a spider walk down the stairs of a D.C. townhouse. The kind of behavior that made people in the Middle Ages and modern-day Catholics call a priest to their house. That's never been a quality I was looking for in a spouse."

I really didn't want to go to the doctor. I really, really didn't. I would very nearly rather stay home and take my chances with major muscle spasms and communicate by typing with a straw in my mouth than go to the doctor. If I had a doctor who would figure out the issue, write me a prescription for whatever ails me, and let me be on my way, that would be one thing. But I don't have that kind. I have the kind who is one of those "above and beyond" physicians, one who wants you to get a little something extra for your co-pay, whether it be some extra facts to put in your cap, a field trip, or a recipe for bran muffins. I guess it could be considered "going the extra mile," but I don't see how that's a benefit when *I'm* the one who's running it.

I suppose putting out even a bit of extra effort these days is all very nice, but when I came down with an intestinal malady that I knew I needed medical attention for, I just needed a quick visit, a prescription for Cipro, and to go back to bed. And, in fact, he didn't write me one prescription, he wrote me two, and told me I needed to go down to the first-floor library to fill them. And then he gave me a recipe for bran muffins, copies of which he keeps in an organizer on his wall, something he had given me on each previous trip for a flu shot, a swollen knee, and eczema.

"Make some muffins! Your bowel movements should have the consistency of a—" he started.

"Ri—" I joined in.

"—iiiipe banana!" he finished.

So, being the rube that I am, I actually found the library, which was oddly not even in the medical facility but off to the left in an outbuilding. I opened the door to flickering fluorescent lights and an otherwise empty storefront filled with bookshelves and tables; it looked more like a used bookstore than a library. I heard some noises from the back, and out from the shadows came a hunched-over figure shuffling toward me. I almost whispered, "Pop Pop?" except that he didn't have any coupons in his hand.

An elderly, very tall man emerged from the darkness. I handed him my prescription and he nodded his head, smiled, and seemed to get very excited. I still had no idea how a library was going to give me pills, but it all seemed to make sense to him, so I rolled with it, and when he told me to follow him, off I went to a corner.

He offered me a seat at a table and I took it. Then he started bringing me books, putting them on the table, and going back and getting more. Finally, he took the seat next to me, dragged a heavy book off the top of the stack, and opened it, with the words, "So this is what diseased intestines look like!"

For the next hour, I looked at picture after picture—some illustrations with transparent layers, some photographs of diseased, cancerous, and pouchy intestines—and the old man, who turned out to be a retired doctor who most likely hadn't seen anybody in the "library" in a number of years, was very happy to see me. It was like he was poring over a yearbook and showing me evidence of his glory days. To be honest, he was having such a good time I couldn't bear to stop him and responded with fictitious amounts of glee when I saw a big, punchy tumor in a colon and pockets of diverticuli dotting some poor guy's bowel.

I guess you could say we bonded a little as I looked through all of the old books with him, trying to think of interesting questions like "So can a tapeworm really poke its head out of your butt?" and "Is it possible to stick a can of hairspray up there, or was my best friend's doctor ex-husband lying about that, too?" and "Do you remember seeing anything at Harvard that looked like a Fart Chart? Officially?"

Now, I wouldn't say that it was the worst hour I ever spent in my life, but being a polite hostage to a lonely old man exploring the mysteries of the poop chute is not at the top of the list of things I'd like to repeat. In addition, the only "prescription" he could fill was disturbing images found in crusty old books, and I still had to go to Safeway and stand in line behind contagious people anyway. And this was in the forefront of my mind the next time I needed medical treatment, when my tongue turned green and I was convinced it was rotting from gangrene, or most likely from simple overtime. I was panicked and took the first available appointment the following day.

And that took a lot of will. Not just because the last time I visited my doctor I was sent as a sacrificial lamb to the medical library, which I would say somewhat shattered my trust in prescriptions—I mean, this time I got an old doctor when I was expecting a nice, easy painkiller; next time I might think I'm getting my high-blood-pressure pills but get a life coach wearing tie-dye instead—but because I had already suffered mouth indignities and I wasn't eager to repeat them. I had been to the dentist twice the previous week concerning a new crown I had installed (since they cost as much as appliances and I am going to start referring to them in the same manner) after the tortilla chip incident. My dentist also thought it would be a great idea to cast a mold of my mouth for a teeth-whitening tray, a procedure that took five of the most paralyzing minutes of my life and caused me to apologize aloud for my Mach 4 gag reflexes.

I was so tired of people sticking their hands in my piehole that when a basket of bread sticks was placed on our table one night when we went out to dinner, my hand immediately flew up to cover my mouth and my shoulders began rolling.

So while I wasn't that thrilled with submitting myself to another oral exam, the green-tongue thing was really freaking me out. It had begun to transform several days earlier, showing hints of a lime sort of color; the next day it dove into a deeper colorway of olive; and by the third day, when hints of brown began to appear, I picked up the phone. I brushed my tongue, I gargled with mouthwash, I rinsed with salt water and peroxide. The color kept sliding deeper into the hues of decay and decomposition, and I was afraid to let it go any longer. Actually, I was terrified that I would be talking and my tongue would flip out of my mouth and land at my feet like a dead fish.

Imagine my irritation when the first thing my doctor said after I opened my mouth and showed him my dirt patch of a tongue was, "Hmm. Show that to your grandmother."

"What?" I asked after he removed the tongue depressor.

"Show that tongue to your grandmother," he said. "Ask her what a Hairy Tongue is. It used to be quite common."

"What does that mean?" I asked, even more horrified than I was when I thought my tongue was rotting.

"Means you've got a Hairy Tongue," was his reply. "It'll go away, just wait."

"I don't want to wait," I replied, and stuck out my tongue again. "Burn it off. Tell me you have a torch in here."

"Do you eat enough fiber?" he asked.

"Yes," I assured him.

"What are your bowel movements like?" he continued. "They should be like a ri—"

"Ripe banana," I finished.

"Here's a recipe for some bran muffins," he said, plucking it out of the organizer on the wall. "Get ripe."

On the way home I contemplated whether I could seriously live with this Hairy Tongue in my mouth or if I should try to look into prosthetics. I didn't want it in my mouth. I still didn't know what it was, how I got it, or when it was going to go away.

I was upset about it all day, and I didn't know how I wasn't going to chew it off in my sleep at night. I looked at it again before I went to bed and brushed my teeth and was just repulsed. I couldn't sleep with that brown slug in my mouth. Here I was, trying to make my old smoker's teeth whiter, and now to have this filthy rug in the middle of them.

And that's when the lightbulb went on.

The next day, I waited patiently, patiently, patiently, and as soon as the clock struck 9:00 A.M., I picked up the phone and dialed.

"Dr. O'Hara's office," the receptionist said.

"Hi, this is Laurie; I was in there just recently," I explained. "I got a crown, and when Dr. O'Hara was trying to match the crown color to the rest of my teeth, he brought out that little ring of teeth-tint samples and I asked if they were all from dead people?"

"Okay . . ." the receptionist said.

"I'm a gagger?" I added. "Like, relentless gagging when the mold tray was in my mouth?"

"Oh," the receptionist said. "Laurie Notaro. How can I help you?"

"Will the teeth whitener turn my tongue snail colors? Like from lime to olive to brown?" I asked.

"Sure," I was told. "If it can change the color of your teeth, it can change the color of your tongue, especially if you're using the tray overnight."

Now, I don't blame the doctor for not knowing that my Hairy Tongue wasn't hairy after all but that I was turning it the colors of death because of the chemicals I was putting on my teeth. But he did scare the shit out of me, and when I asked Nana what a Hairy Tongue was, all she said was, "That sounds disgusting and I have no idea what that is. Don't use my bathroom the next time you come here."

So when I broke my toe smacking it against the cast-iron back bar of my elliptical machine, I rolled around in pain with a purple little piggy that got swollen so bad I could only wear slippers.

And I stayed home and practiced prairie medicine, which would be to frame the situation as "You live alone on the prairie with your ma, pa, and two sisters, and you have broken your toe. What do you do?" And the answer is almost always "Will a bran muffin make that better? Then leave it alone."

Now, I can't say that I was thinking that as I was walking back from the bathroom to the bedroom in the middle of the night and catastrophe struck. I was almost back in bed and was standing alongside it when I stepped on Barnaby, my geriatric cat, who by this time was too old to jump up onto the bed and slept on the floor in a pile of my clothes that I was too lazy to hang up. It is well documented that the cat and I had an adversarial relationship, particularly concerning chocolate stars, but not really to the point that I wanted to snap his spine in half like a twig. I knew for a fact that I stepped on him and was terrified I had horribly hurt him, but I had my earplugs in and couldn't hear if he had screeched or not.

Without pause, I reached down to see if he was okay, but just like that, I felt a terrific blow to my face, and my head jerked back. I fell forward onto the bed, both hands covering my nose as I entered the most primitive state I have ever known (including Ambien) and began emitting deep guttural noises that I couldn't control, let alone stop. Suddenly a hand was on my back, pulling me up, and I opened my eyes to see my husband's terrified expression, which was anything but reassuring. Quickly, I realized that I had not been at the side of the bed but at the foot of it, and in the dark and half asleep, I had smacked the underside of my nose directly on the edge of the footboard.

Blood had already begun to seep through my fingers when my husband pulled my hands away from my face and gave me a towel.

"We need to go to the hospital," he tried to say calmly. "I think you should put your pants on."

I shook my head.

"Yes, we need to go," he insisted. "We need to have a doctor look at your nose. I think it's broken."

"No it's not," I gasped. "It's fine."

The last thing I needed was someone touching my frigging nose. No way anyone was getting near it. Even to have someone *look* at it would hurt. It was like I'd been hit with a two-by-four in the facenuts, if such a hideous, horrible thing existed. I just wanted to lie down and have the pain dribble out of me.

"It sounded like the crack of a baseball bat," he said.

"It's not broken," I mumbled again.

"It sounded like a hatchet chopping into a tree," he continued, making me more and more unlikely to agree to put pants on.

"You can't make me put pants on," I said firmly. "And if you're foolish enough to try, you should know that my toenails are extra long right now."

He backed off like an attentive husband should and left me alone. I curled into a ball while my nose bled, sure that when I woke up in the morning I was going to look like a proboscis monkey with a facewiener, or—for less of a *Nat Geo* and more of an E! reference—Owen Wilson, and I was going to have two huge black eyes.

But the next morning my eyes were fine and my nose hadn't swollen up, proof that I hadn't broken it. I didn't need X-rays or some resident sticking a hand on either side of my head trying to show off. I couldn't breathe out of it or touch it, but my nose looked fine, despite my husband's prodding again that I needed to go to the doctor.

"A bran muffin isn't going to make this any better," I reminded him. "Prairie medicine. Besides, it's not broken. No black eyes."

"If you sneezed, would you pass out?" he asked me.

"No," I said truthfully. "But it would kill me."

My nose wasn't broken. I knew it wasn't. It was just bruised inside, I told myself, and that's why I couldn't touch it for two months. But one day, months later, when I was checking out my teenage-boy mustache in the mirror from different angles, I got a good look at my nostrils. My once perfectly symmetrical nostrils—and, yes, I know it's a little odd to boast about your perfect nostrils, but they were the only pair of anything that matched on my body and would make me the optimum model for a nasal-spray ad—were no longer mirror images of each other. Not only were they no longer twins and my Plan B as nostril model was dashed, but they were even off center, and the right one was all squished as if it was Stevie Nicks's when it collapsed under the weight of an eight ball.

So it appears that my nose was indeed broken, but when you step on a cat—who was absolutely fine, by the way—you can never predict what's going to happen. Your cat could deglove your leg with one swipe, or he could disfigure your nostrils forever. And I thought if I could suffer through that and just have a weird nostril, prairie medicine was my new MO. The results, after all, were the same as going to the doctor, and I never had to put pants on. I felt the whole experience was economical, convenient, and showed traits self-sufficient, even if my mortality rate had skyrocketed.

But with blood pumping out of my foot from the stab wound with the scissor, I knew my prairie-medicine streak had ended. Tetanus was too big of a foe to chance, although the thought of spider-walking in front of my mother in a nightgown held irresistible appeal.

In the waiting room at the doctor's office, the nurse came out and called my name. I got up and walked toward her with a slight limp, ready to get my bran-muffin recipe.

I felt ripe.

It's a Bomb

"**W**ell, I don't know what to tell you," my mother said over the phone when I informed her of what time my flight would land in Phoenix. "That's the same time we're going out to dinner. And this place is nowhere near the airport."

I hadn't seen my family in six months, since Christmas. And while I didn't exactly expect a ticker-tape parade to erupt at my arrival, I also didn't expect that I'd be taking a cab ride that cost more than my plane ticket to my parents' house, simply to sit on the steps in 110 degrees like a yellowed newspaper and wait for them to come home.

"Call your sister; maybe she can pick you up," my mother said. "This restaurant was on *Diners, Drive-Ins, and Dumps,* you know that show? It's an Italian place, but the guy with the white hair said it was good. He drives around to all kinds of crappy places and eats there, so he should know. We can't change it. It's too late. I already made the reservation."

"For when?" I asked a little angrily.

"*Well, I was just about to call them,*" she replied.

In my mother's defense, it was her birthday. She had a right to go anywhere she wanted to go. In my defense, I was flying in to surprise her for said birthday, a monthlong plan that went suddenly awry when she had apparently not really made reservations at the same time my flight landed and my father, who was in on my conspiracy, put her on the phone to tell me.

"I'm sorry," my dad said when my mother gave the phone back to him. "Blame the chunk with the albino head. She saw veal parmigiana on television last night, and frankly, there is no stopping it now."

But that's my family for you. My grandfather spent two years in France and Belgium as a medic in an army hospital in World War II, and when he finally came home—after marching across several entire countries, trying to save lives of soldiers, sailing back across the ocean on the *Queen Mary*, and taking a cab to Brooklyn after the ship docked—he found the house empty. My Nana and my mother, whom my Pop Pop hadn't seen since she was a couple of months old, simply weren't there.

"It was dinnertime," my Nana explained sixty years later as she shrugged. "My father called and said supper was on the table. What was I supposed to do? Everyone was waiting for me. Pop Pop was late!"

It goes to show that in the genome of my family, nothing can fight against the lure of tomato sauce and melted cheese; the mere presence or mention of food has Jupiter's gravitational pull and cannot be stymied. Not even a prodigal patriarch—after helping stop the Nazis from world domination, thus rescuing humanity from having black cheese infested with mites on every menu and reclassifying "cutlets" as "schnitzel"—could be considered if he came home fifteen minutes late from the war. So I guess I should have been happy that I was just flying in from Oregon to meet an empty house and not arriving after battling dictatorships and triumphing over relentless evil, only to discover that if I had to go head-to-head against a meat-ball, I didn't have a shot.

My sister, it turns out, was more than happy to pick me up, even before she ate, bucking centuries of tradition and her very own primal instinct.

"How do you deal with staying back home?" she said point-blank as soon as I got into the car. "I had to go over there yesterday to pick the kids up and I only lasted eight minutes. Mom didn't know how to send an email attachment, so I showed her, went through the steps several times, and she still didn't get it. Finally I said, 'Don't you see the paper clip? The paper clip will tell you that you attached a document.'"

My mother, apparently, though searching the email with her eyes, told my sister she didn't know what the hell she was talking about and went on to inform my sister that *she* didn't know anything about attachments, either.

"Oh, I don't, huh?" my sister told me she protested. "Look right there. That paper clip proves that I know how to attach a document. I do *so* know how to send attachments!"

"There's no paper clip!" my mother replied. "You keep talking about a paper clip and there's no paper clip!"

"The paper clip is right here," my sister said, pointing her finger and showing my mother on the computer screen. "It is *right here*."

"Oh," my mother suddenly said. "You mean the little 'g'?"

"Does it look like a little 'g' to you?" my sister asked me as we flew down the freeway.

"Then, right as I got to the front door, making my escape, Dad asked me if I knew how to recover emails on his computer," she said. "Apparently, he keeps all of his emails in his trash folder, and mom went through it yesterday and deleted them all. He was very upset because he said if he wanted to get rid of them, he would delete them himself, and now they are all gone. Every important email that he never wanted to throw away in his trash folder is gone."

"Why was all of the important email in his trash folder?" I queried.

"Why are you even asking that?" she replied furiously. *"How is a paper clip a little 'g'?"*

I nodded. I got it. Coming back home and staying with my parents did take some adjusting, I have to admit. Even though I left home a long, long time ago—in a move that included defiantly throwing my clothes into the backseat of my car and driving away, before Lady Gaga was born—the second my suitcase rolls into the tiled foyer, I feel as though I've got crow stuck between a crown and one of my last remaining real teeth. And that's because in my parents' house, the parents are parents and the children are still very much children.

I have found myself asking if it was "okay if I had a cookie" before dinner, and I've noticed distinctly that, after being out, I try my hardest to act sober in front of my parents when *I'm already sober.*

Maybe it comes from years of conditioning from my mother lurking in the shadows as I barely made my curfew as a teenager. When I was a junior in high school, I made the mistake one night of coming home by the designated time but unable to walk, due to the poor decision-making process of an immature fifteen-year-old girl named Laurie, who heard that the boy she liked really liked someone way cuter. My mother, clearly a novice at identifying reality-altered behavior, couldn't wait to pronounce that I was on LSD and that our whole family was in crisis, even though the culprit was an unholy mixture of Tang and gin. Ready to pounce and test me for the signals of LSD on any night thereafter, my mother began her drug research, which included (and was limited to) watching *ABC Afterschool Specials* that Melissa Sue Anderson was in, what she heard on the radio in song lyrics, and from *Helter Skelter,* the only book she read in its entirety from 1976 until 1985, or at least that's how long it was in the bathroom on the back of the toilet. While the data was more than incomplete, that never stopped her from believing that she was qualified to distinguish a person who was hallucinating from someone who was a tumbler away from alcohol poisoning, even though shooting fuel-injected Tang out my nose cured me of drinking for a decade afterward.

"I know what 'Lucy in the Sky with Diamonds' is about, you know," she'd say, taking the last drag from her cigarette as she sat at the kitchen table when I walked through the door. "You're not foolin' nobody."

"That's weird, Mom," I said as I got some milk from the fridge. "I thought you boycotted Beatles albums when they stopped wearing ties and you couldn't see their earlobes anymore."

"I bet you think you could fly to your room, don't you?" she replied, and then oddly flashed me a peace sign. "How many fingers am I holding up? Or are you too spaced out to count?"

"I wish I was on LSD, because then this would be hilarious," I said tiredly, as if I really needed to remind her that I was a white middle-class dork who still passed football-shaped notes to her friends between classes and who had no idea where to get underwear that didn't have flowers on them, let alone psychedelic substances from the neighborhood recreational chemist.

"You don't shoplift, do you?" she asked me, grinding out the butt as I chomped on an Oreo, trying to ignore her. "Because shoplifting is just a hop, skip, and a jump to joining a cult. One minute you have a free lipstick in your pocket, and the next thing you know you're carving a pinwheel into your forehead. AND GODDAMNIT, DON'T HITCHHIKE!!"

Even decades later, as an adult bunking with my parents, just asking where the bath towels were might prove to be a dangerous game and could transform me into a ten-year-old in seconds flat. The first time I stayed with them as a taxpaying, car-owning, weed-pulling home owner, who had already experienced her first cancer scare and who wanted to take a shower, my mother simply shook her head. "Here we go," she said with an exhausted sigh, her nightgown riding up terrifyingly higher than her tennis outfit in the seventies, even though my mother still has the legs of a showgirl (a very short Italian showgirl, but even so, it's my mom). "I'm telling you right now, if you're going to take a shower here, this is not a hotel. I'm not cleaning up your hair that's all over the place in the bathroom. If you're going to shed, *pick it up*. Hair makes me gag. All I need is one look. Don't pretend that you don't know that. That's why you're not allowed to bring food over on holidays, only drinks."

When I responded to her "hair talk" with a blank stare—mainly because I hadn't taken a shower in her house since I was twenty years old, my shedding patterns have most likely changed in that time, and also because I was afraid that if I moved my eyes the delicate position of her shorty nightgown might have shifted into a danger zone—I clearly made her more angry. I expected buttons to pop off her nightgown placket and ricochet off the walls or my apparent bald spot.

"You know it skeeves me!" she said as she dumped a towel into my arms. "I'm not picking up your hair and neither is my cleaning lady Patricia! The last time I went into a bathroom after you left it, I thought some monkey war had happened in there!"

"*I was using Sun-In then, Mom!*" I protested with a sneer. "*You* spray that shit all over your head and see what your scalp manages to hang on to! Everyone knew it! Even the FDA! Kmart should never have been selling it!"

Frankly, it wasn't just my mother who had difficulty with the transition of having her daughter return for a week. I don't think my Dad was ready for me to come back home, either. I think it had been a long time since he was forced to make conversation at the kitchen table over coffee, especially with the person who had been canceling out his vote in every single election since the mid-eighties.

"So," he said with a chipper, good-morning smile. "That president of yours doesn't seem to be able to cough up his birth certificate."

"Dad," I said, my eyes still half closed, being that I had been awake for eight minutes. "I don't even have a bra on yet. Maybe we should save the birther debate for Mid-Morning Snack Time. Give us something to live for."

"All right then," he agreed. "I noticed from my office window that you parked facing the wrong side of the street yesterday afternoon for fifteen to twenty minutes, at about four, four fifteen P.M. You know you're going to get a ticket for that. Everyone on this street obeys the law."

"Dad," I said, now that I had been awake for eight minutes and fifteen seconds. "No cop has ever set foot on that asphalt, and if they have, it's because someone saw a car driving down the street that was a model older than 2005 and they panicked."

"Your mother deleted all of my very important emails," he started again. "I had them all filed in my trash folder, and if I had wanted to throw them away, they wouldn't have still been *in* the trash folder. Do you know how to get them back?"

"I wouldn't have the slightest idea," I said, knowing it was unwise to tackle that debacle with or without underwire support. "But if there's anything you can do to get her to stop wearing the shorty showgirl nightgown, I'm all for it."

"Damnit," he said, wincing. "I'm gonna have to call The Geek. Gonna have to call The Geek. Did you know they found the Garden of Eden in Iraq? It's starting to grow back."

"I don't know how hard Glenn Beck was crying when he told you that," I said, getting up and throwing my napkin onto the table in a feeble act of surrender. "But you might want to get a second source. I'm going to go pull my hair out in the shower now."

"Oh, Jesus. Just don't let your mother see it" was all he said.

But, to be perfectly honest, my mother didn't really know what to do with me at the breakfast table, either, although she does wear pants on the first floor of the house, so it was a much safer atmosphere.

"You broke my coffeemaker the last time you were here," she said after she sat down and took a sip from her mug.

"You know that just isn't true. I didn't really break it," I replied. "I just put the water in the wrong hole. It dried out by the time I left. You used it this morning and sixty percent of the coffee stains came out of the dish towels. It's like the space shuttle of coffeemakers. It's far more complicated than it needs to be for an appliance that can only make one cup of coffee at a time."

"*And my coffee is never stale now,*" she said adamantly. "It's an anti-stale coffeemaker."

"Really?" I replied. "Where are you going between the time you put the filter in your old coffeemaker and the time the dripping is done? Are you going into the bathroom, or are you bending the time–space continuum? Where are you going? The

Civil War? American Revolution? If it takes you so long to go to the bathroom that it makes your coffee stale, I hate to tell you, but the issue isn't with the coffeemaker. *Eat more fiber*. Ripe banana."

"I told you to watch the tutorial," she volleyed. "You don't just open a coffeemaker and pour a gallon of water in the first hole you see. It's not a girl at the bar."

And then she gave me a "you know what I'm talking about" look.

"Sorry, that's the way it works with coffeemakers that don't come with a DVD and a certificate of completion. And it's a mystery why you bought a coffeemaker that uses the special coffee packets you can only get on QVC," I shot back. "They look like Chicken McNugget dipping sauces. I still can't figure out if I got the sweet 'n' sour or honey mustard latte."

"I'm getting a new hip," she said, changing the subject.

"You just *got* a new hip," I reminded her. "You haven't even sent Barack Obama a thank-you note for the first one yet. So when did QVC start selling body parts? Is this one bedazzled with Diamonique, or does it have a lighthouse embroidered on it? Are you getting a Joan Rivers hip? Please tell me you're getting a Joan Rivers hip!"

"I'm getting my *other* one done," she informed me, and I remembered all too well the incident of the last hip replacement the year before. Pre-surgery, she got ready for it like a mama bird and began assembling her Recovery (Vicodin) Nest. She moved into my sister's old room, where she had set up a television, a fold-up dining tray, a recliner, and a patio chair, which my father had informed me that she called "the visitor's chair," to which he commented without pause, "Oh, yeah, they're lining up around the block." In essence, my mother had established her very own assisted-living apartment within her very own house. The hospital also gave her a hook hand on a pole—the Gripper—with a squeeze handle at the bottom of the stick to control the opening and closing of the claw.

"Are you getting another Gripper?" I asked. "So when your skin grows back together as one sheet and your transition into the Bionic Woman is complete, maybe you can get some whaling or seasonal migrant fruit-picking work?"

"I don't think that's funny," my mother said. "I hate that friggin' lemon tree in the backyard. Who the hell needs all of those lemons? Why can't it just give me one or two lemons a week? That's all I need. I should stop watering it."

"Are you bringing your visitor's chair back into your apartment?" I asked. "I noticed you moved it in front of the sink in the bathroom. Actually, I didn't notice it as much as realize that I was going to have to get a running start and pole-vault over it if I wanted to get to the toilet."

"It takes a long time to dry my hair with the blow dryer," my mother replied adamantly. "Standing the whole time makes my hip very tired." This was a woman who, if asked what was the single most important possession she would save from a burning house, would answer her handicapped-parking permit or her Ambien bottle, so the chair in the bathroom shouldn't have come as too much of a surprise to me.

"Maybe we should buy you some Sun-In," I replied. "Cut down on your beauty time."

"Why would you keep an important email in a trash folder?" my mother said suddenly, throwing up her hands. "That's like keeping your checking account in the toilet bowl. Right? Right?"

I shrugged, knowing better than to touch that beehive, so I turned matters to the only subject my mother and I couldn't possibly argue about: her grandsons, my nephews.

"You know, I can't believe how tall Nick got," I said, referencing my nephew who had suddenly sprouted five inches since I had last seen him at Christmas. "I feel like someone switched him out with a random mall kid wearing a McDonald's uniform; did you bring him back after a spin on your Time Traveler Toilet? I don't know why we didn't keep him in a terrarium so he could only grow as big as his surroundings would allow. Remember his little baby teeth? I want his little teeth back. You'd better return this version before he sprouts a mustache and our Future Family decides to keep Little Teeth Nick!"

"Oh, if you think his teeth take some getting used to, you should see the hair on his legs!" she said, dropped her voice to a whisper, made a disgusted look, and pointed to her deodorant place. "He even has hair . . . other areas. Like under his armpits. I'm trying to talk him into shaving them."

"Mom, do you want to turn him into a drag queen?" I balked, horrified that he might have even considered asking other boys his age if their grandmas were helping them shave their armpits, maybe even buying them pink razors that they might pop out in the showers after PE, thinking that it was perfectly normal because Grandma said so. "Oh my God. You need to stop that. That's what happens when we mature. We're animals, Mom; mammals get hairy! What did you expect?"

If my mother had hind legs, she would have reared up on them and then kicked me in the face with a front hoof.

"I," she quickly informed me with a pointed finger, "am not an animal. *You* are an animal! *I* read the Bible! *I am not an animal!*"

And with that, her chair left tire tracks on the tile as she pushed away from the table and stood up.

"By the way," she said as she walked away and gave me one

last look, "your shirt is too small. You look like friggin' Pooh Bear."

I looked down, and it was pretty much true. My mom had probably used a vast amount of restraint not to voice that observation as a breakfast opener.

But, to be honest, even *that* revelation couldn't prepare me for what I saw one afternoon a few days later when I walked through my parents' front door after parking my rental car in the wrong direction on the cop-free street. I don't know how my mom and dad didn't know I was there—I had to unlock the door, so I know I made noise. I was making noise, I tell you! But as I came around the corner from the foyer, I saw my mother sitting on the chair with her leg extended, and my father kneeling on the floor, a shoe in his hand. There they were, my parents—who, to my knowledge, had never even made eye contact, let alone touched—and here he was, slipping a shoe on her foot. What was going on here? They both turned and looked at me in the same second, their eyes wide with unexpected horror and shame. I'm sure the look on my face was no different.

No one said a word. The silence actually echoed.

I'm so glad this didn't happen when I was six, I thought as I turned and fled up the stairs, not stopping until I closed the guest-bedroom door behind me.

"—and he was putting on her shoe! They both turned to look at me. Their eyes. *Their eyes!*" I cried quietly into the phone to my sister.

"Oh. My. God," my sister replied in a horrified whisper. "You should really come and stay over here."

"She was on the couch," I said again. "With her bad-hip leg sticking out—"

"SHUT UP," my sister demanded firmly. "SHUT UP SHUT UP SHUT UP!"

"How am I going to go back downstairs?" I asked. "How am I going to face them, after seeing what I've seen?"

"Stay upstairs!" my sister warned. "Don't leave that room. Do you have enough snacks to get you through until morning?"

"Oh," I said, on the verge of a full-fledged panic attack. "I have a bag of chocolate Twizzlers and two protein bars in my suitcase from my book tour in 2008. I won't make it until sundown. Wait—"

I suddenly spied a red bag that was on a chair and could be one of two things: Godiva chocolates from my friend Lucy, or handcrafted, beautifully scented bath bombs from my friend Kathy Monkman. I held out hope for the chocolates as I crossed the room. I knew that Lucy had not only included truffles in her bag but also dark-chocolate-covered almonds, which feasibly could be enough protein to keep me in the guest bedroom until my flight left in two days.

But as I got close enough to the bag to touch it, I smelled the wonderful aroma of flowers, and, though heavenly, that doesn't smell like Godiva. Still, just to be sure, I looked into the bag, and that's when I definitely saw the two delicately packed boxes with the rounded spheres of bath bombs covered in white powder, each resting in a white paper cup. There was no mistaking them.

Bath bombs.

"Never mind, I accept it. I'm going to die," I told my sister. "I left the chocolate downstairs. Please remember me as forty pounds lighter. But if I toss the keys out the window, will you come over and put my car in the right direction? I'm afraid Dad is going to write me a 'citizen's arrest' ticket for aggravated parking. And if I never see you again, check Nick's armpits for stubble."

As soon as I hung up with my sister, however, I heard my Mom yell from downstairs.

"Laurie?" she called.

"I only want to talk about it with my therapist!" I called back.

"We're going to dinner at Outback! Do you want to come?" she replied.

I actually thought about it for a second, because who passes up a free steak and baked potato? But then the reality of spending the next hour and a half attempting to avoid the "Sometimes Mommy Can't Get Her Shoes on By Herself and That's Perfectly Normal Only Because She Has a Bad Hip" talk would cost me more in trying to cure the residual twitching and spontaneous sobbing than a free baked potato was worth, even with all the fixin's.

"No thanks," I shouted back. "You know it's only two forty-five."

"Your father likes to order off the day menu," my mother yelled. "Are you sure you don't want to come? We gotta hurry. The lunch special is only good for fifteen more minutes. After that, everything goes up two dollars."

"Nah, I'm good," I called back, sighing with relief when I heard the front door close.

When my father sat down at the kitchen table the next morning after I had just taken my first sip of coffee and announced, "You know, Anderson Cooper is waging a war against Christmas," I knew that I was most likely in the safe zone and that the jarring "touching incident" from yesterday would not be discussed, just like every other traumatizing family event. Which is exactly how we like it. Everything was back to normal and completely ignored, no matter what the residual effects. Nobody touched nobody.

Until an hour later, when I was ironing the dress I had planned to wear that day and there were two quick knocks at the door.

I was about to say, "Hang on a second," and grab a robe, a shirt, a towel, or anything that would have covered me up, since I was only wearing a vintage full slip—which is legally considered underclothes—when the door swung open and there stood my father.

"He—" He stopped abruptly in mid-word when he saw the look on my face, which I'm sure was the same face I use when people walk in on me when I'm using the toilet (I have now used that face exactly three times in my life: The first was at SXSW, when a girl burst into the stall I was occupying and demanded that I get up because she needed to pee "real quick," and I would have punched her had my underwear not been wrapped around my ankles. And the other time, when my nephew was a toddler and every room was free range for him. Between seeing me in a compromised situation and my mother wanting to Nair the Y chromosome off him, that child has had plenty of deep-rooted RuPaul-level damage).

There I was, wearing basically a long bra dress with my fat old-lady arms naked and exposed, my bra straps visible, and I didn't even have tights on at this point. I looked like every little old Italian widow, except I didn't have food stains on me yet. The only thing that stopped me from slipping into a psychotic break was that, in the event of my developing an alter personality, it would take my father longer to close the door.

"—eeyyyyyyyy," he resumed, in the same amount of time it has taken for comets to crash into the Earth, species to go extinct, established civilizations to collapse, and the world to completely forget that the Romans invented indoor plumbing.

"Good job with the parking," he said. "I can see you're making an effort."

"Okay," I forced out. "I do have a bra on, but I would prefer to talk about this when I'm actually wearing clothes."

"You should really come and stay over here," my sister reiterated over the phone three minutes late.

"I'm leaving tomorrow," I said. "I might as well stay here. I have a feeling Dad's been working hard on a lecture about the Lie of Global Warming, which he plans to present tomorrow at seven-thirty A.M. at our Breakfast Assault. I think he has diagrams, and earlier today someone was printing out pictures of polar bears dancing on a beach and nuzzling with seals. I guess the world isn't perfect. If it was, Milky Ways would only have one gram of fat and Tim Burton never would have made a musical."

The imperfection of the world proved itself a minute later when I walked into the bathroom to dry my hair.

"Mom!" I cried. "Where is the salon chair? The salon chair is gone! I can walk straight through to the toilet! *Where is the salon chair?*"

"I had to move it; it's Thursday," she called back from downstairs. "Patricia and the cleaning ladies come today."

You have got to be kidding me, I thought angrily as I plugged in the hair dryer. Now I have to stand up while I blow-dry my hair? I don't want to stand up while I blow-dry my hair. The thought of it is just exhausting. Standing up is ridiculous! Who does that? Who does that!

"What are you doing up there?" my mother called again.

"I'm drying my hair," I replied indignantly. "And I have to do it upright because *it's Thursday!*"

"Don't make a mess! Patricia will be here in ten minutes!"

she replied. "I know you're up there making a mess with all of that goddamned hair!"

"I am not!" I shouted back. "I am not making a mess! I am rolling up a big ball from all the hair that fell out of my head this week, and I'm putting it on your toothbrush like an ornament on a Christmas tree that Anderson Cooper doesn't want you to have, right at this moment!"

It had only taken a week, even without sitting on my mom's Time Traveler Toilet, for me reset the clock and become twelve years old.

The following Sunday, after I'd returned home, my mother didn't even say hello when my father asked if I wanted to talk to her and then handed her the phone.

"What the hell was in that goddamned red bag?" she demanded immediately.

"Mom," I said. "I'm fifteen hundred miles away. Did you buy a Joan Rivers webcam on QVC and think I can see you? Because I can't see you through any of the holes in the ear portion of the handset."

"The red bag you left here," she explained. "You left it upstairs with all of that other stuff."

"Oh," I said simply, trying to remember. Point is that I never fully embraced the fact that my suitcase does not possess the magical powers of a Lion, a Witch, or a Wardrobe, and cannot carry the contents of a magical, mysterious land within it. Add to this the fact that I live in a land where Soysage is available in convenience stores on any corner, but if you try to buy the only kind of ricotta legally allowed by your mother for lasagna or tortillas that don't "expire" for half a year, you're out of luck, as well as room in the suitcase. As a result of filling it up with cheese and starches, a couple of things got unknowingly left behind.

"Oh," I said slowly. "I'm sorry, I forgot to ask you to mail it to me."

"Mail it to you?" she said sharply. "*Mail it to you?* Why don't you tell me what the hell it was?"

"In the red bag?" I asked. "The one with the ribbons on it and—"

"*I don't know if it had friggin' ribbons on it or not,*" she snapped. "But I do know that when I bit into one of those god-damned little balls, it disintegrated like sand all over my tongue and started fizzing up like acid! I tried to spit it out and it wouldn't come off, and when I drank water it started foaming more!"

"Kathy Monkman's bath bombs?" I asked, even though my jaw was hanging open. "You ate Kathy Monkman's bath bombs?"

"*What the hell is a bath bomb?*" she shot back. "I opened up the bag and there were these two little boxes with balls of candy! They smelled sweet! I thought it was marzipan!"

"Marzipan?" I asked. "Marzipan? Where would you even find marzipan after 1910?"

"There was powdered sugar on top!" she insisted.

"That was baking soda!" I cackled. "I can't believe you ate Kathy Monkman's bath bombs!"

"I didn't *eat* them!" she denied staunchly. "I took a bite! Then it melted, the bubbles started, and I had to lean over the sink and let the froth build-up drain from my mouth. While your father watched. I'll never forget that taste. Never! It was disgusting!"

"Well, I've never seen anyone on *Top Chef* make anything out of borax, Epsom salts, and baking soda," I agreed. "You were approximately one chemical compound away from eating crystal meth. But maybe throw in some tuna and cream of chicken soup and it would be excellent."

"I can't believe your mother ate bath bombs," my husband said from the other end of the couch as he shook his head. "This is better than the time your sister ate the dog cookie."

And that was true, it was better than the time my middle sister found a bag of treats I had just bought my dog, Maeby, from the gourmet pet store. My sister dug into them, uninvited. After she ate the whole thing, I walked into the kitchen and she took that opportunity to tell me that "Those cookies weren't very sweet!"

"You mean the ones shaped like a dog bone?" I replied, noticing the open bag, which was cellophane with little dog bones printed on it; and it was tied with a ribbon decorated with paw prints.

"They had frosting on them," she argued, as if I was somehow wrong and I had mistaken a Mrs. Fields for a pet-supply store with leashes, pet-odor remover, and puppy pads.

"The frosting provided even more detail that it was a dog bone," I informed her, looking into the bag. "You ate the one that had *Woof!* written on it."

Yet my mother had beaten my sister in consuming the unthinkable, because she had identified as delectable edibles not even objects digestible by *any* species, but bathroom cleaners and ant killer.

"Wow, Mom," I said to my mother over the phone. "Tell me what you *wouldn't* eat if you thought there was sugar on top of it."

"They were in candy cups! In candy boxes!" she protested. "All fingers pointed to candy!"

"Oh, no," I corrected her. "No. All fingers were pointing to your mouth. I'm going to leave all kinds of stuff around your house now to see if you will eat it. It will be like an Easter egg hunt, but sometimes foamy. Sometimes not."

"You're so funny," my mother responded sharply. "For a ten-year-old."

"Oh," I replied. "You got that right."

Why Not Take All of Me?

So I was just informed that there's a thing that can block your private parts in X-ray scanners. You know what I'm talking about: the Rapiscan machine that can not only see through clothes but can show how much saggage my multiple decades—despite preventive measures and expensive body butters—have inflicted on all parts affected by gravity and all the unnecessary time I spent not lying down. I know for a fact that Rapiscan is installed at the Phoenix airport, and since I go to Phoenix a lot, I will eventually be instructed to take a trip through the tunnel of horror, which will not only rip my clothes off faster than a guy just released on parole but I'll be STANDING UP. And I get a nice, single-serving dose of cancer for an amuse bouche.

I thought for a moment that I would absolutely have to get these little things called Flying Pasties—tiny patches you can adhere to your "no access" areas to ensure privacy—and I was scrambling for my credit card when I suddenly stopped and thought, Why am I doing this? TSA, if you want to peek in my pants so badly, go right ahead. If you really need to invade my privacy the way you claim because some underachiever on a flight to Detroit tried to light his wiener on fire, you deserve what you get.

And that's not all.

You really want to see me naked, let's take this baby all the way. Take a good look, because if it's so important to get to third base without even buying me any sort of dessert first— preferably chocolate-filled or anything on fire—shaving is off the table. If you're looking for a belly ring, I'll give you a jelly ring instead. It's that thing that folds over. And you'll be getting the bra that has one strap held to the cup with a safety pin, because that's the one that doesn't dig into my back fat so much. And underwear?

If you're sure you wanna buy a ticket to no-man's-land, get an eyeful. Drink it in, my friend. No, that's no loincloth, those are the panties that I save for Midol days, with the torn waistband and an aggressive stubbornness that OxiClean couldn't conquer. And yes, that just might be fire shooting at you out of my nipples, drawn in Sharpie, and when I turn around, those just might be the words "KISS IT" and an arrow pointing to my ass, which no human eyes have seen since 1994.

Until now.

Enjoy.

And don't worry. I'll be back.

Show Ho Ho Time

❦

The moment I walked into my neighbor's Christmas-perfect living room, I felt inadequate.

I had never seen a Christmas tree in a non-retail situation look so pristine; the wood-stoked fire in the fireplace roared heartily, and the aroma of a freshly baked ham drifted all around us. The décor was so perfect that I expected Diane Keaton to waltz through at any minute, wearing all off-white cashmere. I wasn't sure how my husband and I were going to work our way into the mix, but we were going to try, and I suddenly felt very lacking about the Christmas wreath hanging on my door, which I had cobbled together like a craft mom from fir and cedar debris that had crashed into my yard during the last storm.

Being new on our street, we were thrilled when our neighbors invited us to their holiday gathering, since we were anxious to get to know the people in our community. We had already encountered some of the folks on our street, but this was a chance to not only get to meet a wide variety from around the neighborhood but to show our hosts that we were friendly, personable, and nice.

Martha, our hostess, was welcoming and warm and showed

us into the kitchen, where the holiday goodies had been spread out. Careful not to appear as either gluttons or too picky to enjoy the food that she had obviously gone to a great deal of effort to prepare, we took a little of this, a little of that, and tried to mingle. It was a house full of people that we had never met before, which is not easy when you're limiting your drink to apple juice to ensure that "the new neighbors across the street desperately putting on a good front" don't become "the alcoholics that just moved in, let the house go to shame, and are probably selling drugs, because she's home all day." We met the retired lawyer from up the street, whom I had seen walking his min pins several times a week; the librarian, who was the star in the senior-center holiday program; and a young wife who was there with her husband and really didn't know a soul, either. She, however, was slightly less concerned with first impressions than I was, evidenced by the nearly empty wineglass in her hand. That is foolish, I thought. *Glug, glug, glug!* This is a neighborhood holiday gathering, not a bachelorette party. You need to be on your best behavior. This is showtime, lady!

A half hour later, disaster struck. We had just finished nibbling on our ham and snacks when Martha came into the room and made a sweeping cull, choosing people here and there without any indication of criteria. Somehow, my husband escaped, but I wasn't so lucky. With Martha's hand at my elbow, I was guided into the living room with the rest of her picks. Once she had herded us in front of the piano, she had a helper hand out copies of the "Jingle Bells" lyrics to the guests, and she sat down behind the keyboard. I had been wrong.

This was showtime.

Oh, how I wish I had not only forgone the apple juice but had downed several shots. I am simply not a singer. I do not come from a family of singers. When we get together and warble "Happy Birthday" to one another over cake and candle, it doesn't sound as much like a song as it does a pack of jackals yapping over a fresh carcass. And in my case, it's nothing that you want to inflict on the innocent, or at least on people who haven't reported us to the city yet. Who is flat, off-key, or tone deaf in the Notaro clan is all up in the air—it doesn't matter, and we can't tell, anyway. The fact of the matter is that we all know it, and instead of choosing to come together as a family and embrace our difficulties, we have formed splinter groups, which then mock the available "talent" in the other splinter groups. On holidays, to the naked eye it will look like everyone is carrying on, singing a jolly tune, but if you pay attention, the sound is suspiciously thin. It becomes clear that 80 percent of us are lip-synching it, leaving only the people who have married into the family and the children, who aren't aware of their hideous, hawkish voices yet, to round out the song.

Therefore, I wasn't too happy when I was handed the lyrics and Martha began to tinkle out some notes. I didn't realize I was going to be expected to perform; the invitation certainly didn't say anything about mandatory vocal contributions. In addition, I didn't know why everyone wasn't asked to join in, only a handful of victims. Why would you go and pick people like that instead of just plunking one note down on the piano and letting all of the guests who had the performer chromosome come running in seconds flat?

The young wife that I had met in the kitchen had also been picked and stood next to me. We exchanged similar glances of pity, each wondering what we had done to make ourselves stand out.

Martha finished her intro and launched jovially into the song, and I noticed that many of the singers possessed robust voices, like the librarian who was starring in the senior-center program. After pretending to get lost on the words of the first line, I feigned a laugh, acted a little goofy, and launched into the song myself.

Albeit silently.

But I was pretending to have a good time, even using my pointer finger to make sure I followed along with the right words, looking at the other singers, making my eyes smile thanks to Tyra Banks, and nodding my head when I felt the moment required an extra dash of jubilation to make it real. And, just for the record, this was new for me. No one practices Facial Song Acting in my family; we all just look pissed and hungry until the song is over.

But with "Jingle Bells," I was starting to actually enjoy myself and feel that I was an active part of the choral community, when the music stopped unexpectedly and the lyrics came to a sudden screech, trailing off like water buffalo running off a cliff. The whole party got quiet. And when I looked up to see what had happened, I saw Martha, and Martha was staring at me.

I felt my face turn flame red.

"Laurie," Martha said in front of everybody, "are you mouthing the words?"

If anyone didn't know who I was before, they sure did now: I was now the Word Mouther. Song Ruiner. The "Jingle Bells" Liar. Everyone's eyes bore down on me. The white-wine new friend next to me took a step aside and cast shame in my direction.

"Listen," I wanted to say. "I didn't ask to sing. I didn't want to sing. You made that decision for me! You marched through this party and picked people at random, like a Broadway version of Dr. Mengele. 'You sing!' 'You sing!' 'You just watch!'

I'm just trying to appease a hostess and not harm my fellow neighbors. There's something that comes out of these pipes, all right, but it's not the gentle tweet of a songbird. It is the sound of gears grinding the flesh and bone of inner ears."

But I didn't say any of that. Instead, I stood there, caught in the silent spotlight, with even my husband watching, and said, "Yes."

"Oh, no," Martha responded immediately. "This is a party, and we all need to sing."

"I'm sorry," I apologized.

"Jerry," Martha said, as she pointed to an older man in a Fair Isle sweater and motioned for him to take my spot, "I need someone here who can deliver."

"Laurie," she added, looking back toward me as Jerry plucked the lyrics sheet out of my hand, and I halfway expected her to send me to the party principal's office to wait there until they all decided how to deal with me.

"Come next to me," she said, carefully thinking, then handed me a tinkly object she'd grabbed from the top of the piano. "You can be on bells."

I smiled as if I had always wanted to be on bells, as if I had been eyeing the bells from the minute I walked through the front door and finally they were mine, or as if I would have jumped on the chance if I could have majored in bells in college.

Satisfied that I was now within striking distance, Martha smiled politely, counted to three, and jumped into the intro again. I smiled as I watched all the singers do what I couldn't and waited for Martha's signal for my foray into the song. She gave me one firm nod on the chorus, and I jingled my little heart out. Jin! Gle! Bells! Jin! Gle! Bells! Jin! Gle! All! The! Way! Oh! What! Fun! It! Is! To! Ride! In! A! One! Horse! O! Pen! Sleigh! EY!

It was like the whole party took a collective breath when they saw I was going to shake the bell for real and not just move my head and murmur, *"Ching ching ching."*

A! Day! Or! Two! A! Go! I! Thought! I'd! Take! A! Ride! . . .

I felt like I was a contribution to the gaiety of the evening, to the holiday atmosphere, and was being a worthwhile party guest. I was chiming along, lending so much festivity to the party, when the music stopped abruptly again, this time only long enough for Martha to hold up her right hand and sharply inform me, "Only on the chorus, dear," before she led her troupe back into the second verse, which I had apparently been busy mutilating.

There are four verses to "Jingle Bells," in case you didn't know, and when sticklers sing the song in its entirety—which they tend to do when they've written out every single lyric on a sheet and copied it off on party paper—it can last longer than *Avatar*.

When we finally finished the song, Martha smiled again, took the bells from my hand, and thanked me. My husband had my coat already waiting for me at the front door, and my bell hand begged for my wrist splint during the short walk across the street. We never mentioned to each other, although we both knew that the next time we moved to a new neighborhood we were going to have to work up a routine or obtain a circus skill before accepting any invitations.

A year later, my husband and I were bundled up on a Tuesday night and were going out to get a bite to eat when I noticed something strange. There were cars parked everywhere, up and down the street, in front of our house, almost blocking our driveway. I had never seen that many cars on our street before. And that wasn't all.

It was like a scene from a movie. People were streaming from every direction, also bundled up in hats and scarves, carrying pans, trays, and sometimes gifts, and all were converging on Martha's house. If I didn't know better, I'd say a team of horses pulling a sleigh had parked at Martha's curb, delivering several ladies who'd been nestled under tartan wool blankets.

From my porch, I could see through her living-room window: The house was already packed. The perfect Christmas tree had been resurrected, and a fire blazed on the hearth. People were milling about inside, and I'm sure they were chewing on ham.

I looked at my husband at the same time that he looked at me. I opened my mouth to say something, but I was too stunned to make anything come out.

"Don't even tell me you're surprised," he said to me after he locked our front door and stood in front of it.

"I can't believe she banned us," I whispered.

"WELL, I CAN," my husband mouthed.

And it was true. We had been blackballed from the neighborhood holiday party, that was it. No second chances, no replays. One episode of lip-synching and we were sunk. No pleas or explanations of why I was faking it would ever be heard. I had apparently insulted my host by not participating in the fullest holiday sense, and I was not going to get a reprise.

I really tried hard not to take it personally, and I suppose that it stung that much harder because I liked Martha and her husband, I thought they were nice people, and my feelings were kind of hurt. Yes, I am a jackass who tried to lie my way through a Christmas carol. Yes, I am the neighbor who spazzed out on the shaking of bells and evidently took it too far. Yes, I am the one who would completely mouth the words again if given the chance, because if my hostess thought that was bad, she should have heard the damage I could have done with my lungs activated and at full blast. People have reacted more calmly to air raid sirens than they have to my singing voice. And here we were. New on our street, already outcasts. I hoped that it was a misunderstanding and maybe this party wasn't the same sort of party as the holiday party last year; maybe this was a party that we wouldn't fit in with, much like the parties we had had full of graduate students. Maybe this was a party strictly for the senior center, I tricked myself into thinking. And then, in the window, I saw a different neighbor chatting with another guest, a neighbor that wasn't a member of the senior center or anything like that. The neighbor was just a neighbor. And I had to admit that we weren't invited because I was just me.

I had failed the audition for "fun neighbor."

We didn't get invited the next year, either, or the year after that, but by then, whenever I saw a stream of jolly, happy holiday people descending on Martha's house, the sting wasn't quite so sharp. I had learned to expect it.

And then one day in December last year, Martha rang our doorbell.

My husband answered it, and she asked if he might be free to help move a heavy table for her. He said sure, and when he came back, he mentioned that after he had helped move the table down a flight of stairs, Martha looked at the space in the living room where the table had been and exclaimed, "This year, we'll have room for dancing!"

I looked at my husband intently.

"Really?" I asked. "She said that?"

He nodded his head.

"What do you think that means?" I prodded further.

"Well," he began, "I think it means there's going to be some high kicks over there some night soon."

"Did she say anything about an invitation?" I queried.

"No," he replied. "But I have a lot to do today. I didn't stand around and make small talk."

"Maybe she'll put the invitation in the mail, like last time," I wondered aloud.

"We weren't invited last time," my husband reminded me.

"I mean the time we were invited," I said, a little irritated.

"I don't know," he said honestly. "I wouldn't count on it."

"Well, who would ask someone over to move heavy pieces of furniture to make a dance floor and then not invite them to the party?" I asked. "No one would do that. I think we're back in. We have to be back in. Right? Don't you think? Wouldn't you feel bad if you didn't invite someone who helped you? I would. I felt bad when the UPS lady delivered the turkey and I didn't invite her over for Thanksgiving. We're back in. We have to be back in!"

My husband just shrugged. "I moved a table down some stairs," he replied. "I didn't go to Israel and initiate peace talks."

That following Thursday, there was indeed dancing at Martha's house. People were breaking out moves you typically only see at weddings with an open bar. It was a good thing she moved the table; she really did need the room. I had to stop a couple of times because I was laughing so hard I could hardly breathe, especially when my husband went for broke and delivered a David Lee Roth high kick that missed a lamp by millimeters.

To be honest, I hadn't had that much fun in a long time. We danced a little, ate some snacks, and I single-handedly brought "Jingle Bells" back, at the top of my lungs, for all to hear.

I sang it loud and proud, until it annoyed my little dog so much that she jumped up and attempted to push me down, while my husband used the fake sleigh bells from this year's storm-wreckage wreath and accented Ev! Ery! Sin! Gle! Syl! La! Ble! In the chorus AND the verses.

Far away and across the street, I doubt anybody at Martha's had such a good time.

Chill Out, Grass Lady

To tell the truth, I had walked up into the house through the front door and had gone back to the car three times in the course of the day before I noticed something was wrong. When it finally hit me that things were not as they should be in front of my house, I stopped dead in my tracks and gasped dramatically, "You have GOT to be shitting me!"

Frankly, I don't know what other reaction you could possibly have once you realize two trees have been stolen from your yard.

The two trees, on either side of my porch in enormous pots, were gone. Simply gone. As in not there. The enormous pots were still there, but the trees themselves—two beautiful azaleas with fuchsia-colored flowers that had just exploded into bloom—were no longer planted in them.

I stood there and stared at the porch, speechless, looking for the trees. Because as anyone who's had anything stolen from them will tell you, the first reaction you will have when you discover your thing is gone is that you will look for it. As in, "Certainly my eyes deceive me. Humanity cannot be so depraved that someone would thieve up to my front porch in the dead of night and steal two trees from my yard. I have overlooked them taking a break from being potted trees and they are in lawn chairs sunning themselves on the north side of the yard, because I'm sure it's frustrating to be a tree and never be able to go anywhere, suffering from Restless Trunk Syndrome."

And no matter how many times you've been stolen from, the reaction is always the same: disbelief. Complete and overwhelming shock to the point that if you go out to the street and your car has been stolen, if there is a fire hydrant within the general vicinity, you will look behind it. Because you cannot believe it. Getting robbed, it seems, never gets old.

As it turns out, this isn't the first time that I've had live goods plucked from within inches of my front door. I'm actually a veteran of plant crime. On Mother's Day a few years ago, some asshole waddled up to his mother's house with a ceramic pot full of pincushion flowers and Miracle-Gro potting soil that I had purchased from Home Depot merely eighteen hours before. It hadn't even cleared my bank account yet when D. B. Cooper jumped off my front steps holding my planter, scurried to his getaway car—which, remarkably, wasn't registered to me—and showed the jackal who bore him that although he couldn't be bothered to stop in at Walgreens to get a friggin' card and a stuffed animal, a son's love is always worth making a rap sheet a couple of lines longer.

That morning, I even looked behind the folding chair I also had on the porch for the twenty-pound pot of flowers, just in case I had misplaced it.

But you know what? There's no misplacing trees. I mean, you can gasp and shake your head all you want, but you'll never find your tree under a paper towel on the coffee table or behind a loaf of bread on the kitchen counter. It wasn't like they were hiding in the mailbox or stuffed behind a solar light.

When I finally recovered enough to speak, I yelled to my

husband to come outside quickly, and when he did and I explained what had happened, the first thing he did was look for them, too.

"The trees?" he said, his eyes darting from corner to corner. "They took the trees? Are you sure? How does someone steal trees? They were as big as you. They were as tall as you are!"

And then, since I'd had extensive and thorough detective training because *Law & Order* was Nana's favorite show, I began to search for clues. Yet, oddly enough, there weren't any.

"This is creepy," I said to my husband, pointing to the facts of the case. There was no soil spillage. The area around the pots was completely clean. It was as if the trees were surgically removed, as if someone used a laser.

"It's like a cattle mutilation," I dared to whisper, a little bit in awe. Frankly, I can't pull a tomato plant out of a four-inch pot without spraying dirt in a five-foot radius like a soil-filled jack-in-the-box, so I could only come to the conclusion that whoever helped themselves to my trees had some sort of extraordinary method of extraction.

"This was planned," my husband said, who had a couple of *Law & Order* marathons under his belt, as well. "This wasn't a random shrubbery theft. This was a deliberate hit."

"You know, I'm inclined to think that," I said, almost laughing. "But in this town that would mean we were insinuating that a couple of hippies got together and coordinated something more complex than who was bringing the pot and who was bringing the bong."

"Believe me, I know how impossible it sounds," my husband agreed. "But this was planned. There's no way someone drove by here at three in the morning after the bars closed, noticed that we had some particularly lovely trees, and happened to have a shovel and tarps. I've never known a drunk to choose digging over a three-for-a-dollar taco run. No, this was brazen. I highly doubt these were the first trees they've abducted. Now it's your turn to say something snappy, Len."

"Yeah." I nodded. "Why would drunks steal trees when three blocks away there are still two street signs left on High Street?"

"I guess we'll never know what kind of person steals trees," he said simply, clapped his hands together once as if the case had been solved, and went inside.

But I had an idea.

The tree theftery wasn't the first such ridiculously bizarre event to happen in my front yard, and this wasn't even the same front yard where my potted flowers had been stolen. Several months earlier, my sister was due to pull into the driveway with her son and my brother-in-law for a visit, when my little dog, Maeby, went nuts over something she spotted while standing guard at the screen door. My sister had never been to my new house before, and I knew that whatever went down during their vacation—good, bad, and downright ugly—was going to be in the full debriefing report she would supply to my mother upon her return home. After which there would be a phone call from my mother, who was still quite upset that I had moved beyond running distance from her, and who would delight in telling me that her suspicions about my new abode were absolutely confirmed, relaying that "Your sister said there were weeds in the cracks in your sidewalk, you still haven't learned to vacuum, and your dog isn't as smart as you said she is."

Thinking my sister had arrived early, I went to the door and took a peek outside but saw nothing and chalked it up to a taunting squirrel. Five minutes later, Maeby went nuts again, and this time I walked out into the front yard for a more thorough investigation. It didn't take more than three steps to see what was causing the commotion.

There, in my fertilized, mowed green grass, was a heap right under the biggest tree in the yard. A heap of human. It was wearing a hoodie, baggy pants belted basically at the knees, and a backward baseball hat. Initially I wasn't sure how to proceed, but I marched right over to the tree and hoped that I would figure it out once I got closer.

The heap, it turned out, was a guy, lying on his back, his skinny legs bent up, and his arms splayed wide across the grass. He had not been there five minutes prior when Mae alerted me to the presence of an intruder, but he was there now, sprawled out in my yard with less than ten minutes to the touchdown of my sister. He was a young guy, teens, maybe early twenties, but no older than that, I decided, as I looked at his bony, angular, and paler-than-any-pale-should-really-be complexion. But I stopped wondering about the drained color of his skin once I saw an ant crawl across his eyelid.

And then another ant. And another ant.

Now, to say that a swarm of ants was marching across his face may be a bit too suggestive, but I have to emphasize that "swarm" is a relative term when creatures have more than two legs and they appear in multiples. To me, that's a battalion, and to make matters worse, when they're invading a landscape that happens to be a face, there's usually only one reason for that: The face is on a corpse.

My stomach flipped and a curtain of horror dropped on me.

" . . . and your sister tells me that when she drove up to your house, there was a dead person in your yard!" I could hear my mother dig. "Who has a dead person in their yard? No normal person has a dead person in their yard! There is not one single person in my neighborhood who ever had their sister visit when there was a dead person in their yard! EVER. Why do you have dead people in your yard? Do you think it's funny to have dead people in your yard? Well, let me tell you, your sister was *very* upset! And it's not funny!"

I had approximately three to four minutes to move the carcass from my yard into my neighbors' yard so my sister would think it was *their* dead person. But, ever the optimist, I decided to hope against hope and resuscitate him with the power of fright.

"Young man," I commanded loudly, as I stood over him and the kingdom of the ants. "*Young man!* Are you all right?"

While there was no outward response, I realized that he absolutely had to be alive; his knees were still bent, his feet flat on the ground, and again, citing my *Law & Order* training, I knew he certainly hadn't been there long enough for rig (shop talk for "rigor mortis," FYI) to set in. And as far as the phrasing is concerned, I frankly have no idea where within me "young man" came from, except that I suppose nothing terrifies a young vagrant as much as an old lady armed with a cane and a cordless phone that has the cops on speed dial.

But he didn't budge. He didn't flinch. An ant sauntered across his nose.

"Young man!" I attempted again. "Who should I call for you? Should I call your caseworker, should I call your sponsor, or should I call your parole officer?"

The ant traipsed around the rim of the left nostril, then wandered over toward the right one.

" . . . because I can just as easily call the police," I added. "And their number is shorter."

And who knew that those words were so magic that they could roll a boulder away from the mouth of a cave and the dead would suddenly awaken.

"Whuuuut?" the kid mumbled, raising himself from the dead as his eyes fluttered open despite the swarm of insects establishing a colony on them.

"I asked you if you needed me to call your parole officer or the police," I clarified. "Because it appears you may be in some form of distress."

Now, it's true and I will be the first to admit that there have been times in my life in the not-too-distant past when I have woken up in strange places—like on a friend's bathroom floor, where I landed after I fell off the potty and horked on the wall during the way down the night before my college graduation ceremony because I got too friendly with a bottle named Jack. However, I never, ever, *ever* decided that someone's yard looked like a very good place to lie down *in broad daylight* after I had been up for five days while smoking meth out of a pipe with a crust of battery acid on it.

"No, I'm fine," he barely spit out as he finally rubbed his eyes. "I'm good."

"If you're so good, why are you unconscious in my grass?" I demanded, towering over him, my hands on my hips.

Two minutes and counting.

"I'm not," he said—still, I might add, lying down. "I'm cool. I was just walking down the street and it looked like a good spot."

"A good spot?" I asked. "A good spot for what?"

"To sleep," he said, almost as if I was stupid for not figuring it out.

"Well, you need to get up," I informed him. "You need to be on your way."

"Why?" he asked incredulously.

"Because you can't sleep in my yard," I explained firmly.

"Really? Why not? It's just grass. Grass belongs to everybody," he shot back in a very snotty tone, as if the problem was me, as if the issue was that I thought I was just too good to have a random tweaker, after being awake for the better part of a month, collapse in my yard on his way to the bus station, drool in my grass, and let my bugs crawl in and out of his orifices while he slipped into an exhaustion coma—all as my sister took pictures and immediately emailed them to my mother while she was attending to her duties as a Eucharistic minister at church.

"That is so funny, because I didn't get your contribution this month to pay for the fertilizer, water, or the guys to come and mow the People's Grass," I informed him. "This is private property, which means, in People's Terms, 'not yours.'"

"Maybe I'm not done sleeping," he replied.

"Well, if I call the police, they have this amazing wake-up toy that will solve that problem," I reminded him. "It's called a Taser."

That made him sit up.

"So who do you want me to call?" I asked again. "Your caseworker, parole officer, or the police?"

"I'm getting up," he said, and he shot me a dirty look with his tiny pinhole pupil eyes as he wobbled to his feet. "I'll find another place."

"Not on this block you won't," I said with a shake of my head. "Two streets down there are trashy people who have had a couch on their curb for three months now. It's the People's Couch. Go sleep there."

"You should chill out, Grass Lady," he said, as walked down the street with the legs of a newborn calf.

"Oh yeah?" I said, leveling the field, and then quickly added, as if my mother was whispering in my ear through an earbud, "I can call the police if you don't feel okay! 'Cause you don't look okay! Mister!"

"I'm okay!" he yelled back, and gave me a very discourteous wave of the hand.

"I know you're on drugs!" I yelled. "I can tell! Normal

people don't collapse in strange yards and fall asleep! You should try doing that in the woods in Germany in a witch's front yard and see what happens to you! You're lucky you didn't wake up in a cauldron! Because I have one!"

Then I realized that it is never a good idea to piss off a drug addict whose rationalization skills aren't as sharp as they could be, even though I seriously doubted Hansel could find his way back to my house with a handheld GPS he had just stolen from someone's car. And my cauldron isn't really that big, by the way, only big enough to dump a two-pound bag of Hershey's Miniatures in it and leave it on the front porch for some Type 2 teen dressed as a Dungeon *and* a Dragon to pillage on Halloween.

So even though I'd successfully chased the carcass out of my yard months before, his bony crystal-meth face was the first one I thought of when I ran down the list of possible suspects who might have nabbed my trees. Actually, it wasn't a list; there was just one entry, called "Hansel." But when I really thought about things, I ruled him out: You can't sell trees at a pawnshop, and his muscle-atrophied arms of string cheese probably would have pulled right out of their sockets like a boiled chicken's had he tried to use them for anything except putting a test tube up to his lips and flicking a lighter.

I, however, was still struck by the insidiousness of the treenapping and was examining the crime scene when I heard someone walk up behind me.

"That is just terrible," I heard my neighbor Gloria's voice say as I turned around. "And they were in full bloom. Terrible time to uproot a tree."

"I can't believe anyone would steal trees," I said, dumbfounded.

"There was a rash of plant robberies last year on the next

street," she informed me. "We thought the worst was over. This is clearly bringing it all back."

I was puzzled. "I never heard anything about that," I said, surprised. "When was the last theft?"

"In the fall," Gloria told me, and I nodded.

"No one wants a tree that's going bald," I surmised. "But who doesn't want a tree with a healthy headful of purple hair? I think the plant bandit has rebloomed."

"Did you follow the trail?" Gloria asked, motioning toward the sidewalk.

"There's a trail?" I said, getting immediately excited, to which Gloria pointed.

"Right there on the sidewalk. It's not much, but it is dirt, and it leads right up the hill," she confirmed.

And sure enough, there was a line of soil—admittedly not a direct line, but a clump here, a splash there, definitely soil that had fallen from something being hauled up the street, which amazed me. The perpetrator was so brazen that there wasn't even a getaway car or an escape wheelbarrow. The whole exit strategy involved pretty much nothing but one asshole dragging two trees by the neck up a hill. And I guess that in a place like Eugene, where I routinely have to wait for a person lumbering on stilts or carrying a ferret in a BabyBjörn to cross the street before I can make a left or right turn, not much fills the definition of "out of the ordinary"; a guy only hauling two trees with fresh dirt still clinging to the roots could have feasibly been the mayor or someone elected to the city council.

"I'm going to follow that trail," I told Gloria, and I did just that, stomping my way up the hill, guided by a patch of black soil here and there. Gloria followed close behind and pointed out the trail when I became stumped several times. I finally stopped when there was no more dirt to be seen and the clues abruptly dried up in front of a house that was in need of a weed whacker and a paint job. In Eugene, that's a sign that whoever lives inside does own a cauldron. Full-size.

And that is right where my plan of action came to an abrupt halt. I looked at the house and didn't really know where to go from there. Did I knock on the door and ask if they had seen my trees? Did I call the police and attempt to press charges because the dirt stopped in front of their house? Did I try to peek in their windows to see if I spotted any fallen purple leaves? I didn't have any proof, I didn't have a description, and I didn't even have a picture of my trees to prove they were mine in the first place.

I was standing on the sidewalk with Gloria when I heard a familiar voice call out my name. It was Roy, our realtor and friend, who lived a block or two up the hill with his wife, Patti, who'd sold us our house. He was just starting his daily bike ride when he saw us, slowed to a stop, and asked me how I was.

When I told him about the theft, his jaw dropped and he said he was sorry to hear it. I explained why we were in front of this particular house and why I didn't exactly feel confident about taking the investigation any further.

"Those azalea trees were beautiful," he said, shaking his head. "They were in full bloom. I had heard that there was a plant pirate in the neighborhood last year, but I thought that was all over."

"This is clearly bringing it all back," Gloria repeated.

"I don't know what to do," I said, shrugging and feeling generally powerless. "I guess I'll just have to buy two more trees."

"The nursery has some pretty ones," Roy told me. "I was

there this weekend and saw a couple. They'll run you about a hundred, hundred twenty apiece."

I was stunned. When we bought the house, the trees were a package deal with the foundation and the roof, which said to me that it was too much of a hassle for even the people who paid $120 per tree to take them.

"You're kidding," I said dismally. "So I guess I could replace the trees for two hundred forty dollars, only to have them stolen again? I'm not made of money! In fact, even if I put a cheap little shrub in there, who's to say that won't get stolen, too?"

At that moment, I decided to take a stand.

"No," I said to Roy and Gloria. "I won't be a supplier for someone too cheap to buy their own plants. I'm not going to put anything back in the pots. I'm making a point. I have a message to send! Whoever stole my plants walks down this hill and up this hill every single day. They looked at those trees and waited until they were in their prime to abduct them, and they're waiting for me to replant them so they can pillage my porch again. And I'm not going to play that game. On the way up the hill, they're going to have to look at what they've done, and they're going to see it again on the way down the hill. Empty pots. Nothing but empty pots. I'm making a statement! I can't afford to keep feeding some evil person's tree habit!"

And honestly I was very happy with my decision, even though after about a week or so Gloria came over to ask what I thought I might replant in them, as did almost every neighbor on the block, even ones I hadn't met yet. Every time I wandered outside, someone popped over or came running across the street, anxious to know what I was planning on planting in the empty pots. It almost seemed as though I was creating more of a disturbance than the person who ripped my trees off in the first place.

"I was thinking," my neighbor Sue said as she caught me outside weeding what I loosely term the "flower bed," "that maybe some nice hydrangeas would look just perfect in those pots."

"Well, I do think you're right, but I'm going to leave them empty," I tried to explain. "I'm making a statement to whoever stole them."

"Oh, that's right," Sue said, nodding. "Gloria mentioned that you couldn't afford to replace them."

"That's not exactly what I said," I started, but Sue had already begun to walk away.

"Petunias can be nice," she said over her shoulder. "They're not expensive, but they are awfully common. . . ."

Still, I stuck to my guns and steadfastly refused to replant anything. The pots stayed empty for a long, long, long time. I definitely wanted the goblin who thought they could help themselves to my foliage to know that the stock had been depleted and their crime spree was over, at least in my yard.

Then, one day in almost fall, I went outside to pick up the paper and, lo and behold, there were two bushes freshly planted, one in each pot. And there was not a drop of soil on the ground. Again, in the dead of night, someone had snuck up to my porch this time delicately placing two deep-green shrubs with brilliant red berries on either side of my door.

It was now the third weird thing that had happened in my yard.

I pressed each of the neighbors, particularly Sue and Gloria, and all of them denied it, although by the looks on their faces, the relief had been as long coming as if the empty pots were equivalent to not only a People's Couch in my front yard but a People's TV, which is also down the street.

The good deed went unclaimed. I questioned friends, Dave the mailman, Eva my UPS lady, and still no one would fess up.

Until one day my husband and I decided to wander downtown and go to a food fair, and we weren't there five minutes before we ran into Roy.

"Hey, how are you two?" Roy greeted us jovially, and then pointed at me. "What's all over you? Was there an ash cloud that just swept through here?"

"Oh," my husband laughed, swatting at my hair. "I think it's powdered sugar."

"Every time I bite the funnel cake, it touches my head," I said, trying to explain and pretending to be horrified at the size of my fair food snack.

"I heard about the shrub shanghai," Roy said sympathetically to my husband. "That was unbelievable."

"What's even weirder is that a couple of weeks ago, in the dead of night, a little plant fairy brought us some bushes back," I added. "We just woke up one morning and there they were! Personally, I think it was one of our neighbors who was distressed over the disgrace of the empty pots and was afraid the zoning police were going to switch us to the zip code of the neighborhood that doesn't bring their trash bins back in."

Roy smiled. "Well, there might be a plant fairy that lives up the hill somewhere and always has a spade in her back pocket, ready to do good deeds. But I'm not saying if I know for sure or not."

"Has anybody who lives at your house been to Home Depot lately?" I asked Roy, trying to see him around my funnel cake.

He just grinned.

"Maybe, maybe not," he said cryptically, but I knew in that smile that somewhere up the hill, in the form of a spade and a tarp, the good had outdone the bad.

You Give Me Jellyfish Fever

"Nicholas, run! *Run!*" I screamed at the top of my lungs, trying to shout over the deafening crash of the surf hitting the beach as I watched him about to get swallowed by a huge wave.

As evidenced by my screaming on the beach like a demon, our vacation with my nephew had not turned out quite as planned. My husband and I were terrible, terrible substitute parents. When I originally had the idea of bringing Nick up to visit us for a couple of days before my sister and the rest of her family flew up, I had nothing but charming and delightful reveries in my head, and now it was looking like the reality couldn't be laughably further from those trite little dreams.

It's true: Many years ago I assessed the impact of propagating my family's genome even further and quickly withdrew my nomination for motherhood in the general best interest of the world, because I knew I could never guarantee that the hand reaching out and grabbing your leg from the middle of a department store clothing rack wouldn't belong to my child and I get very angry if someone else has helped themselves to my snack food. But that didn't mean we couldn't have a wonderful time with my nephew as we took him to the redwoods to have the vacation of a lifetime. He was almost twelve, and the window of him still wanting to be in the same room with us was about to quickly close; soon, I knew, he would communicate solely through grunts as he discovered, layer by layer, how uncool we were. He had a bag of Chex Mix with his name labeled on it and I had mine, and as long as our hands stayed in the respective bags, everything was fine for the time being. We packed the car up and headed south to the California border, but not before Nick asked if we could stop at the bookstore so he could read a book during the car ride, since he had already finished the one he brought. I beamed with pride.

We stocked up on reading material for all of us, and five hours later the trees got bigger, and bigger, and bigger, until we reached a sign that informed us that we had, indeed, reached our destination.

If you've never been to the redwoods, all I can say is that it really has to be one of the most spectacular places on earth; it's majestic, amazing—every superlative fits. Tree trunks as big as houses, sunlight streaming through branches, and the subtle quiet and absolute stillness blend as wisps of fog rise and roll together to form a place unlike any I've ever been to before.

"Isn't this great, Nick?" I said as we walked on a path deeper into the forest, where everything became bigger and quieter. I expected that at any moment my nephew would begin jumping up and down from excitement as he cried out in joy, "This is the best place I've ever been! Thank you, Aunt Laurie! I love these trees! They are huge! I now have changed my mind and no longer want to be a football player; I want to be a dendrologist, which is a scientist who studies trees, and devote my life to preserving and studying these magnificent, beautiful works of nature! You have changed my life, Aunt Laurie, you have changed my life!"

"This is pretty cool," my husband said as he gently shook Nick by the shoulders from behind.

"Yeah, it's okay," he said.

"It's *okay*?" I said, laughing at Nick's coolness toward it all. "These are the biggest trees in the world. Some of them are thousands of years old."

"The knight in my book is a thousand years old, and he just cast a spell so he can escape a ship he's being held captive on by a king who used to be good but is now a warlord, so I'd like to see what happens with that, you know," he replied as he shrugged, hands in his pockets.

"Oh" was the only thing I could think of to say.

"You know, they filmed part of *Return of the Jedi* here," my husband added.

"That was before I was born," Nick said simply. "And my book is sort of more interesting."

We have three days here, we've been in the car all day, and he's tired, I told myself. Give the kid a break. Let him read his book. Who cares if you just drove eight hours to get here and it's one of the most amazing things you've ever seen? Who cares if he's not into it right now? We have a ton of other things planned: We're taking a gondola ride up the side of a mountain, we're going to the beach, we're going to drive through the Avenue of the Giants, we're going to the Sea Lion Caves, and we are going to have fun.

We are going to have fun.

We are going to have fun.

We are going to have fun.

And we did. Nick had fun reading in the backseat of the car as we drove the rest of the way to the cabin we were staying at, I had fun while I ate the rest of my Chex Mix, and my husband had fun thinking to himself.

When we got to the cabin, Nick decided to change into his pajamas and rifled through the backpack my sister had gotten ready for him.

"Aunt Laurie?" he asked after a couple of minutes. "Do you have an extra pair of pajamas? Mom forgot mine."

"Hmm," I said. "Well, how about you just sleep in the T-shirt you're wearing? Would you be okay sleeping in that?"

"Not really," he said honestly. "Grandma says only hoboes sleep in dirty clothes. Mom forgot my shirts, too. I only have this shirt and three pairs of shorts."

I was shocked. While I wouldn't be surprised if she forgot to pack a toothbrush or comb, it was rather unlike my sister to forget to pack something like clothes. Any of them. While Nick was well stocked on socks and underwear, everything else was missing.

"Are you sure?" I asked my nephew. "You checked everywhere?"

"Yep," he said, nodding.

"Where did she think we were going that you wouldn't need shirts?" I asked aloud. "Alabama?"

I finally talked him into sleeping in the shirt he was wearing—but not before much, much arm-twisting and the agreement that we would get him some new clothes the next day, although I had no idea where. We were almost in the middle of nowhere, and the only thing separating us from actual nowhere was a small grocery store across the street that, while offering live bait and bags of microwave pork rinds, thankfully did not offer apparel of any sort.

Being that the cabin had one bedroom and a small futon in the living room, I gave Nick the choice of whether he wanted to sleep on the futon by himself or bunk with me in the bedroom, and he chose the latter. Even though he was eleven, sleeping in a strange place without either of his parents might be a little bit unnerving, I realized, so I decided not to make a big deal out of it. I was, however, touched that I got to hang on to the last moments of Nick's kiddom, of his not wanting to be quite so independent, and I was happy that those moments weren't all gone, not just yet. We got ready for bed, Nick brushed his teeth, I got my sleep mask and earplugs out, and we all called out good night to one another.

Nicholas got under the covers, snuggled up to the pillow, and I was going to turn the TV off, but I couldn't find the remote control.

"Where's the remote?" I asked him.

"I have it," he said, looking at me. "I need the TV on to fall asleep."

"Are you sure?" I asked, not finding any joy in that news. "Don't you want to just give it a shot?"

He shrugged. "Not really," he replied. "That's why I picked this room with the TV. Because, you know, I thought the futon looked fun."

"Does it have to be ESPN?" I asked. "Could we at least put it on Bravo?"

"I don't watch any shows on Bravo. It's a lady channel," he said decidedly, and without much of a response, I caved.

Remarkably, though, I fell asleep pretty quickly, because the next thing I remember was that someone with Chex Mix breath was shaking me.

"Aunt Laurie," I heard. "Aunt Laurie."

I jolted awake and my eyes flew open immediately.

"What's the matter?" I said, ripping my face mask off and plucking out my earplugs as a shot of adrenaline surged through my system. "What happened?"

Nicholas slowly and cautiously pointed to the ceiling. "I saw a spider," he whispered.

"Are you sure?" I whispered back wearily, my heart still pounding in my throat. "I bet it was just a shadow, honey. Or a fly. I bet it was a fly."

He shook his head. "I saw lots of legs," he confirmed. "Eight. I counted them."

"This is what happens when you keep the TV on," I whispered back as I got out of bed and turned the light on. "When it's dark you don't know that spiders are crawling above you."

But I looked at the ceiling and didn't see a thing, and certainly not a big enough spider whose legs could be counted by a little boy through the flickering light of basketball highlights.

"Right there," Nick said, pointing to a teeny spot on the ceiling on the far, far side of the room.

"That?" I said as I got closer to it, realizing I'd had pimples bigger than the fearful creature. "Now I know why your clothes are missing: Your mother packed your night-vision binoculars instead. You counted the legs on *that*?"

Nicholas nodded. "Eight. That's what qualifies them as arachnids."

"Nick, it looks like a Skittle from here," I argued, grabbing a shoe and climbing onto a chair to reach the terrifying offender.

"A Skittle wouldn't crawl in my ear or into my mouth and lay eggs," he countered, as I whacked the tiny spider and grabbed the carcass in a tissue.

"Is it all right if I flush this, or did you need to incinerate it?" I asked.

"I think you're overreacting," he informed me.

"Oh," I said. "Oh. Well, let's see who overreacts when they

have to wear the same hobo shirt until their mother gets here with her credit card."

The next morning we headed out to the Trees of Mystery, a roadside attraction featuring a mile-long trail through the redwoods called the Kingdom of Trees that is "devoted to the myth and mythology of Paul Bunyan." There is also a restaurant, a gift shop, the sky gondola, and a forty-nine-foot-tall figure of Paul Bunyan and a giant Babe the Blue Ox, complete with Babe the Blue Ox giant "adornments hanging from the lower torso," shall we say.

"Nick," I said excitedly. "Go stand underneath Babe and let me get a picture."

He went over obediently, stood under Babe, and smiled.

"That's great!" I yelled. "Now just reach one hand up and touch the balloons."

"Those aren't balloons, Aunt Laurie," Nicholas told me.

"Yes they are," I insisted. "They just don't have strings, because people would trip on them. But they are balloons."

"I don't want to touch the blue balls, Aunt Laurie," Nicholas yelled back.

"It's concrete," I shouted in return. "They're not real!"

"Please don't make me touch the blue balls, Aunt Laurie," he said. "I don't want to touch the blue balls!"

"Every other kid in this parking lot has touched the blue balls and let his parents take a picture of it," I pleaded. "I promise, when you get into college this will be hilarious."

"My mom wouldn't make me touch the blue balls," he said forcefully.

"Your mother would be over there holding your hands to them," I told him. "When you were three, she took a video of Goofy flipping off the Mad Hatter while you were eating pancakes at Disneyland. I bet she makes this the wallpaper on her computer. Smile like you're having fun!"

Nicholas reluctantly raised one hand above his head and barely grazed the adornments with his fingertips, his mouth curled into a frown.

"Smile like you're having fun!" I yelled. "There's a bunch of other kids behind you waiting to touch Babe's balls!"

I clicked anyway. It *will* be hilarious when he goes to college.

In the gift shop, we picked out several new T-shirts for Nicholas, and I will say I was disappointed when he chose the Paul Bunyan over the Babe shirt, although I did talk him into one with a profile of Bigfoot on it. We then took the sky gondola up the mountain, through the canopy of the redwoods, all the way to the top, so high we could see the ocean.

"Are we going to go to the beach?" Nick asked.

"Sure," my husband replied. "We could go there right after we get back to the car if you like."

"Really?" my nephew said, looking very excited.

"Of course," I said as I shrugged. "Provided that, before we get to the car, you touch the balls again, but with a smile this time."

Heading west in the car, I figured it was the optimum time to impart some words of warning.

"Now, a couple of weeks ago when we went to the coast, the beach had pieces of jellyfish scattered all over it," I told Nick, because the last thing I wanted was for him to poke around at some beach blob and get it all angry. "Don't touch it. I don't want you poking it with a stick, I don't want you covering it with sand, I just want you to ignore it like it was your younger brother."

"Okay, but why?" he asked.

"Jellyfish are one of the deadliest animals on earth," I explained. "If you think touching concrete testes was bad, that's nothing compared to what a jellyfish will do to you. So just do not touch it. Okay? Are we clear?"

"We are clear," he agreed.

As we pulled into the parking lot that was parallel to the beach, Nick's face lit up.

"Wow, I can't believe the ocean is right there," he said as we got out of the car, and he dashed into the sand, kicking it up into the air behind him and running toward the surf. My husband and I followed behind, picking up rocks, pushing sand around with our feet, and examining blobs of jellyfish *from a distance*. I saw Nick stop and stand, watching the waves come in, and when one on the large side was about to hit, I noticed that Nick wasn't moving. He was just standing there, almost like he was hypnotized.

"Nicholas!" I screamed, trying to shout over the grind of the surf. "Nicholas, run! *Run!*"

But he either didn't hear me or was ignoring me, and that wave charged at him like a bull. It broke on the beach, feet from him, and then kept coming until Nick was thigh-high in water, and still he continued to do nothing but stand still.

He waited until the wave drained away before he turned around and started back up the beach, but by that time my husband and I were almost to him. He was soaking wet from the waist down.

"Nick!" I cried when I got to him. "Didn't you hear us screaming to run? Why did you just stand there? Why didn't you move?"

"My shoes got covered in sand when I ran," he said, water dripping from his shorts. "I wanted to wash them off."

"You were trying to clean your shoes off in the ocean?" my husband laughed.

"Nick, you are sopping wet," I said, thinking that it was a good thing we were starting our trip to the Sea Lion Caves that day and had all of our stuff packed in the car. "And, by the way, your strategy to clean your shoes is a little bit off."

The shoes were caked with sand, but it hardly mattered since they were waterlogged with seawater; with every step my nephew took, the shoes oozed and chunks of sand crumbled off.

After Nick changed into a new pair of shorts and his Paul Bunyan shirt in the backseat, we headed toward Oregon with Nick's wet clothes and spongy shoes under the hatchback.

"I can't believe that just when we bought you replacement shirts, you ruined your shoes," I said. "Those will take days to dry out."

"I can wear them," Nicholas said hopefully. "I'll just wear two pairs of socks."

"Sure, and your mother will show up and we can show her your delightful case of trench foot," I replied, but I did remember seeing a Target on our way down. I was hoping we would get to it before we had to stop somewhere for lunch and were turned away with a scowl and a finger pointing to the sign that said NO SHIRT, NO SHOES, NO SERVICE. My theory was that we were at a hearty 50 percent, because we still hadn't lost our standing from earlier in the morning when we had shoes but no shirt. To avoid that scenario, we pulled into a KFC drive-through where my nephew ordered a two-piece meal, plus popcorn chicken, plus an extra biscuit. With all of the food he was eating and the necessity of replacing his entire wardrobe, I wasn't sure how much longer our vacation funds were going to last.

Thankfully, an hour later we approached the Target, pulled into the lot, and parked. My husband and I got out of the car, though Nicholas stayed put. I opened the back door and looked at him while he looked at me.

"Well . . . ?" I asked. "Would you like to join us as we buy you new shoes?"

"Are you going to carry me?" he asked. "I only have socks on."

"Kids your age in Africa are parents already," I replied. "No, we are not going to carry you. You are going to walk in there with your socks on and we're going to pretend that nothing is wrong. We're a Walmart family that ended up at the wrong giant retailer because Pappy used a homemade GPS called a divining rod."

And despite the fact that that was my original plan, I couldn't help but blurt out, sometimes in an inappropriate volume, "I can't believe you thought the ocean would wash your shoes off for you. I just can't believe it," every time we passed another person who had children with them who sported footwear.

We found the shoe aisle, and Nick naturally gravitated toward the most expensive pair, like we were on a reality makeover show.

"We're going to stay in the three-digit range," I reminded him. "You pick out a nice pair someone in India younger than you made with their tiny, skillful hands."

Nick had just tried on a pair of shoes that he liked when he looked at me and said, "Aunt Laurie, I don't feel very well."

"What's the matter?" I asked.

"I have a headache and I think my stomach hurts," he said, looking despondent. "I think I might throw up."

"Oh no," I said in a panic to my husband, and then turned

back to Nicholas. "Do you need to go to the bathroom? Are you really going to throw up? If you're going to throw up, make sure to do it on the aisle and not the rack of shoes, okay? Do we need to carry you now?"

"I bet it's the whole chicken and the gallon of grease he just ate," my husband said.

"It's not," Nick said, shaking his head. "I think it's because of the jellyfish."

"What," I said, looking at my nephew. *"Jellyfish?"*

"The jellyfish on the beach," he said, looking down.

"You did not touch a jellyfish after what I told you in the car," I said quietly. "What did I tell you?"

"That it's the third-deadliest animal on the planet and causes a hundred deaths per year, and I have a better chance of surviving a hug from a polar bear and an encounter with a salt-water crocodile than I do from messing with a jellyfish," he murmured. "And I touched one."

"Explain to me what you did," I said calmly.

Now, because I saw that there was not a whole jellyfish on the beach and just clumps of what *used* to be jellyfish, I really doubted that Nicholas had been stung by a dead pile of goo, but he was an eleven-year-old boy and they will put a hand on anything, especially if it looks like a giant booger. So I tried to remain calm, tried not to believe my own lie that touching a jellyfish was going to kill my nephew.

"I saw a jiggly thing on the beach, and you said not to touch it with a stick, so I kicked it with my shoe," he confessed.

"Okay," I said, taking a deep breath. "And then?"

"And then I thought that I was going to die, so that's when I went and washed the shoe in the ocean, to get the deadly poison off so my leg didn't soak it up," he finished.

"And that's it?" I asked.

"That's it; then we went back to the car," he said, terrified. "I have Jellyfish Fever, don't I?"

"No," I replied.

"But I'm pretty sure I do," he told me, looking worried.

"Nicholas, you do not have Jellyfish Fever," I said firmly. "There is no such thing."

"Are you sure?" he said. "Because I'm pretty sure I feel like I have it. My insides feel that way. Sort of jiggly."

"You don't," I assured him. "Maybe when we get back to my house we'll rent *Food, Inc.,* and you'll understand why your insides feel like they are liquefying. Value Meal Plus Popcorn Chicken and Biscuit Fever is what you have, and it's very similar."

"Are you sure I'm not going to die?" he asked again.

"I'm sure," I reassured him. "I wouldn't lie to you. Again."

"I like the shoes," he said, admiring his feet. "I don't think I could make these."

"I'm glad," I said. "You're wearing them up to the cashier."

"Can I get another bag of Chex Mix while we're here?" he asked. "Someone ate the rest of the one with my name on it."

It's a good thing Nick liked his shoes, because the next morning he was certainly using them. There were quite a number of stairs to the Sea Lion Caves, not to mention the elevator we took down to the bowels of the earth. It's the biggest sea cave in the world, and as soon as the elevator doors open, you know it. The cave itself is open directly to the ocean, with a viewing platform overlooking the vast interior that sometimes has up to five hundred sea lions hanging out on the rocks. And, believe me, there's no mistaking the fact that something that eats fish is living there. Or that a lot of things eating a lot of fish are living down there. Like a town that eats nothing but fish and just throws the carcasses out the front door to ward off evil. It's a powerful, encompassing smell. I'm sure on the odor meter it's officially a "stench," and I was trying my best to ignore it and enjoy myself, but really. Really. It cost the three of us thirty-two dollars, which is a lot for someplace that smells like a Morton's processing plant, and if I'm going to pay that much to take an elevator to a cave that was already there, a cave that the earth made but forgot to equip with a ventilation system, all I'm saying is that a couple of Glade candles wouldn't hurt.

And certainly, once you get to the viewing platform and see the expanse of the cave before you, it really is breathtaking. That's especially true when at the moment you get up to the front of the platform, the biggest male sea lion—roughly the size of an Escalade—lifts himself up to show his full, incredible stature, roars the loudest wildlife noise I have ever heard, pounds his flaps on the rocks a couple of times, and then shoots a tunnel of vomit from his cavernous mouth as if it were a fire hose that lasted a good four to six seconds, throwing up all over the other sea lions lying within a twenty-foot spray radius. I don't know how many stomachs one of those things has, but it's more than one. And it's not just vomit but fish vomit, just a Jacuzzi's worth of sea barf, the smell of which hit us like a pyroclastic flow from the guts table on *Deadliest Catch*.

The response of revulsion from the crowd hit the mark at the same second; a collective "Ewwwww!" traveled around the cave like rumors of an unplanned pregnancy on a field-trip bus. I can't speak for the other witnesses, but the sea lion magic was clearly gone. This was particularly true since the other sea lions didn't appear to realize they had been hurled on, and it seemed a little Tijuana-ish to simply stand and watch mammals roll around in someone else's puke. It turns out that the way you clear out an underage party is the same way you clear out a sea lion cave, and it's always the fattest guy who does it. Needless to say, the ride back up in the elevator wasn't nearly as full of smiles as it was going down; we all had to be very still and focus, because if any one of us gagged, we were all going down. The splash zone in an elevator isn't very generous, and if one person heaved on another, most of us were far enough up the evolutionary ladder to know it.

After driving for a couple of hours, we found ourselves on the main street of a small mining town and spotted what looked like a cute little diner. We stopped and decided to have lunch, thinking it wise after our recent history concerning fast food.

We ordered hamburgers and fries (we all agreed: no fish and chips) from a middle-aged man who seemed very friendly, and as soon as he took our order, he went behind the counter to the grill and started cooking. While the restaurant wasn't exactly hopping, several groups of people finished their lunches and paid the man, who was the only one working there, and pretty soon we were the only people in the diner. When we were finished, we got up and together went to the counter to pay.

As soon as we got to the counter and the man came over to ring us up, the door opened, the bells on the door chimed, and three young men who looked to be in their late teens came in. Immediately, the man behind the counter pointed to the tallest of the guys, the one who came in first, and shouted, "Out! Get out! I told you to never come back in here!"

The guy stood there in front of his two huge friends, all of them small-mining-town kids trying to dress like gangsters.

"You're going to regret it!" the kid yelled at the man. "You think you can fire me and get away with it? You're going to pay for it, you goddamned wetback!"

My adrenaline surged and I felt my entire body turn cold. I

grabbed Nick's arm and pulled him closer to me. I looked at my husband, and I knew he was feeling the exact same thing I was. Definitely unsettled. We were trapped at the counter; behind us was the only entrance and exit, which was blocked by the three guys, and on the other side of the counter was their target.

"Get out of here!" the man yelled again. "You stole from me! I'll call the police!"

The guy shouted an expletive and then called the man a "spic."

"I'll beat the shit out of you," the guy warned. "You'd better watch yourself. You'd better watch over your shoulder every minute of every day. You think you can start shit with me? I'm going to burn your shithole down."

I was frozen; I didn't know what to do.

"Get the hell out of here!" the man yelled in return. "I'm calling the cops now!"

"Go back to Mexico, asshole," one of the other guys added, and then, cued by the tallest one, they all turned and walked back out of the diner.

"I'm not done with you!" the tallest one called over his shoulder as the bells chimed again.

It was silent for a while in the restaurant. The four of us stood there; no one moved. Then the man reached for the credit card my husband had put on the counter when we walked up. He slid it across the Formica and swiped it through the terminal.

"I'm sorry," he said, shaking his head but not looking at us. "I'm sorry that happened."

In moments like this in the movies, writers have had time to figure out what the right thing to say is, what the best way to handle it would be, how to offer some clarity to the situation or even a nugget of wisdom to wrap it all up.

But the truth is that in real time none of that happened. I

didn't know what to say. Nothing came out of my mouth. I couldn't think; all I knew was that I had Nicholas with me and what had happened could have ended pretty badly. I was frightened. I was just glad the thugs were gone, and I was shaking, even though the incident didn't take more than a minute or two. I didn't know this town, I didn't know these people, but I was terrified of them, and I'd never wanted to leave someplace so badly.

"That was terrible," my husband said to the man. "You should call the police."

He nodded, and we left the restaurant and headed directly across the street. I walked quickly, herding Nick in front of me to hurry up and get to the safety of the car. I couldn't believe that those assholes put that in front of my nephew, just a little kid. Put that there and let him see that, let him hear it, a kid who, up until three minutes ago, thought tiny spiders on the ceiling were the biggest things to be afraid of. For what seemed like a very long time in that diner, I had the feeling that we might well end up as Flannery O'Connor characters on vacation. I didn't know what these guys were capable of or if they had anything tucked into their waistbands or not. I had no idea how far their anger would take them. All I knew was if you could bust into a restaurant and start shouting blatant threats and racial epithets—not to mention doing it in front of a child—your range probably knew very little bounds and nothing was off the map.

"You okay, Nick?" I asked.

He looked at me, took a deep breath, and nodded.

"I thought I was going to poop my pants," he said as he reached for the car's rear door, and the honesty of my eleven-year-old nephew allowed the three of us to burst into nervous laughter as we got into the car.

My sister, her husband, and my younger nephew, David, flew into town a day after we returned home. I knew that Nick couldn't wait for them to come, and I couldn't blame him. I mean, here we had promised him this awesome vacation, and, instead, in the last three days I antagonized him into touching fake scrotum, he stood up to a huge wave because he believed he was already a dead man and the sea might as well take him, we ruined his shoes, made him go to the bowels of the Earth to see a giant sea lion hurl, and gave him a front-row seat to his first hate crime.

Great vacation.

The first thing I said to my sister when she got off the plane was, "Nick started a tab," and when I explained to her that she neglected to pack him more clothing than was required for a day, she looked at me like I was insane.

"Look," I said, as I pointed to Nick in his Bigfoot shirt and new shoes. "Recognize any of that?"

"I don't know what you're talking about," she said. "He had so many clothes in that bag I almost couldn't get it closed. Most of his clothes were in the big pocket. Didn't you check?"

And, as it turned out, that was true. There were shirts, pajamas, and pants underneath several pairs of socks and underwear, which, alarmingly, he never used enough of to see what was underneath. How was I supposed to know? I trusted the kid. I figured if you're old enough to go to the bathroom for forty minutes with the door closed and you really *are* just reading a magazine, you're old enough to figure out what a pair of pants looks like folded up.

We headed back out to the coast, where we had rented a cottage near the beach. When we'd unpacked, my sister suggested we take a stroll on the boardwalk that we had just driven past and mentioned something about seeing pedal boats. Frankly, I can't say that I was fan of pedal boats, but if that's what family vacations were made out of, I could use some schooling, unless there was a Nazi Youth rally or a cross-burning happening nearby that I could throw us into the middle of.

My husband and I were first and got into a tiny two-seater; we got a brief lesson on how to direct the rudder and were off for a twenty-five-dollar-an-hour pedal-boat ride. My sister and her family were slotted for the four-seater boat.

"Have fun," my brother-in-law said, waving us off with a smile that was suspiciously too wide as the pedal-boat guy pushed our boat away from the dock. "Remember that I predicted this would be all my fault."

Puzzled, we started paddling. It was a beautiful day, so we just sat back and made it to the far end of the inlet in about a half hour, then made our way back. My sister's boat was nowhere in sight, but I assumed they had headed off in the opposite direction and were doing their own thing. I was pretty sure by the time we all got back to the dock, Nick would have told his parents what an awful time he had with us, how we ruined everything that could have been fun.

But as we got closer, it was clear to see that my sister's boat was only about thirty feet away from the dock. Well, I figured, if you have four people pedaling, you can make way better time than two slowpokes can. My sister's family was singing, and she was standing up and waving something, as if she was leading them in song.

Which I knew was absolutely implausible, given the fact that, on a good day, anyone with our DNA would rather eat one of their own than break into song. Additionally, I understand the call of my own pack, and it was clear that those hyenic yapping noises had a different sort of origin and a far more nefarious translation.

As we approached, it became apparent they were pedaling in circles, over and over again, a result of the rudder getting stuck in one unfortunate position next to my unknowing brother-in-law's leg. My sister, still standing, was shrieking to her husband, who did not look amused, "Pedal harder, Taylor! You are not pedaling hard enough to go anywhere! *God-damnit! Pedal HARDER! Get us back to the dock!*" In her hand was a large piece of blue plastic, which, when she had gotten into the boat, was the back of her seat—until it snapped off in one solid piece as soon as they'd floated thirty feet away. In the rear of the boat, David's whole head was a brilliant red as tears streamed down his face as he repeatedly screamed and sobbed, "We're sinking! We're sinking! There are sharks in the water! *We're gonna die. We're gonna die!*"

And then there was Nick, who, as my sister's family continued to pedal into another revolution, simply looked at my husband and me pedaling quietly by and mouthed one word to us: "*Help.*"

He just might be back again next year.

Please Don't Call China

Dear Whoever Has My iPhone:

I'm sure you thought it was weird, finding an iPhone lying in the middle of the street last night, nestled in its tiny black leather case, just sitting there on the asphalt. I would have thought it was weird, too, maybe even funny. How often do you see something like that? It's almost as common as finding a baby on the street, except an iPhone is a lot more fun to play with.

That's what I would have thought, too, but when I woke up this morning and realized that my iPhone wasn't in my purse, car, or coat jacket, I knew something was seriously, seriously wrong. I jumped into my car and raced back to where we parked last night, and I scoured the street. It was nowhere in sight.

Then my sister called me on the house phone, and apparently you butt-dialed her last night at 2:45 A.M. for three minutes while you walked around with my iPhone crammed in your pants somewhere. If it's still there, kindly take it out. So, I'm sure the first thing you did this morning, aside from moving my iPhone away from your privates—I mean, I don't know how much radiation comes off that thing, but if it's possible that you can kill bees just by turning it on, do you really want to take that chance with things that should stay uncooked in your shorts?—was notice that there's a listing under "Lost & Found" on Craigslist for my iPhone, in which I include not only my email address, so you can let me know that you have it, but the words "REWARD OFFERED."

And I'm serious about that. I could certainly spot you a breakfast for doing something very nice and thoughtful by returning my iPhone; in fact, I'd be delighted to.

How about breakfast and coffee? Even something complicated that Starbucks would charge extra for. Hey, my treat— after all, you're doing me the favor, remember! No arguments!

But I just checked my email, and nothing. I realize it may be too early for you to arise and sober up a little—I mean, judging by the phone call to my sister's, you were up pretty late. I'm sure it will take a couple of minutes for you to figure out you found my iPhone, discover that you desperately want to return it, then run through a series of logical deductions and immediately go to Craigslist, which would be the reasonable place that someone who had lost their iPhone would list a "Lost" ad. "Lost" ad with "REWARD OFFERED," you know. Make sure you see that!

It's okay. I have time. I know how it is. I was in college once and on occasion found myself wandering the streets at two forty-five in the morning, finding iPhones and whatnot that some unfortunate soul had dropped because she was too stressed to realize it was in her lap, not in her pocket, and she stood up and, well, you know the rest, right? iPhone in the street. Oldest story in the book.

So I just checked my email again and I guess you're sleeping a little bit longer, which is fine, it's fine. I'm cool with that. Because I'm sure as soon as you're able, you'll email me and I'll email you back to ask you under what circumstances you found the phone and what my case looks like, because, after all, there is a REWARD OFFERED, and I can't be running around, giving rewards to everyone who found an iPhone last night, you know. And I need to make sure it's not one of those Russian mobster "Meet me at the gas station and give me the REWARD OFFERED first and then I'll give you the iPhone" sort of deals, because you can't be too careful. I have to watch out for myself, although I am quite appreciative of your potential willingness to even meet at the gas station, I sure am.

You're a late sleeper, huh? Maybe you're having dreams about returning the iPhone you found in the street to its rightful owner because that's THE RIGHT THING TO DO. Because I think it's probably pretty obvious that no one would just go out and throw an iPhone into the street and walk away, right? Right? I mean, it's not like anyone has a fight with their boyfriend on an iPhone and gets back at him by whipping the phone out into space like an engagement ring or something. No one would treat an iPhone like that. It's a treasure. I don't know of one person who would. I took good care of it; why on earth would I throw it on the ground? I stood in line for hours to get it. I had my favorite songs on it. Seriously, I had 750 pictures of my dog on that phone, not to mention some private photos I took of myself in a hat I had custom-made for me by a girl named Paula on Etsy, in case you looked. *I know*. I know, it's not a great photograph, I know that. None of them are. But I was trying to look tough and be funny; it's a hunting hat, get it, with a deer embroidered on it? She did a good job with that hat. I still have the hat! That didn't fall out of my lap onto the street. Still have the hat. So, no, that's not what I look like regularly, not at all. I look like that mainly because it is hard to take your own picture with an iPhone; it is not like a regular camera at all. Did you know that? You just have to guess where the button is and keep touching it and touching it around the area you think it might be and, yes, it can get frustrating, and, yes, you can get hand cramps because that's the hand where my carpal tunnel is the worst, so that's why I was yelling in some of those pictures. But I was yelling at myself in those pictures, not at the iPhone and certainly not at anybody else, so it should not be an indication of my character or person, not at all. I'm a nice person most of the time. Eighty percent of the time. Maybe 76 percent of the time. In almost all of my iPhone pictures, *I am being nice.* In fact, if you flip through those photos, as I'm sure you might have—not saying that you don't have any respect for the privacy of the person who was clearly careless enough to get out of her car with an iPhone on her lap, not at all, I'm sure you do, but curiosity baits us all—you'll see that I take photos of happy, jocular things, demonstrating my multifaceted interests, hobbies, and things I see as curiosities.

After all, can a girl who has 750 photos of her little dog— who you may notice is sometimes wearing accessories, such as glasses and hats—on her phone be all that bad? She certainly can't be as bad as someone who doesn't deserve to have their phone returned and loses it to someone who instead does something nefarious with it, right? But, no, you probably won't see any pictures on that phone of me building houses with Habitat for Humanity or volunteering in Central America, holding open the mouths of tykes while aiding Doctors Without Borders as they fix the cleft palates of little children. Probably not on that phone, but I did give them twenty-five dollars once, I just didn't think to take a picture of me donating online. I'm sure it was used to fix a palate. Or at least part of one.

But if you wonder whether I took the picture of the girl sitting on the curb with her butt crack hanging out while her boyfriend was breaking up with her, no, I did not take that. My friend thought that was funny, and in a way it was. She really needed a belt. But even if I tried to tell her, I doubt she could have heard me over her racking sobs.

All right, I took the picture, but listen, it was a once-in-a-lifetime chance, you know? I saw the crack rising up and I just snapped, I didn't even think. It was during the 24 percent of the time when I'm maybe not so nice. It was like seeing the Loch Ness monster or something similar, no one will believe you unless you offer proof. Now I have proof. So when I tell the story, I can offer a visual, and people believe me. That a girl who is very busy having her life destroyed by someone she loved can be too distracted to know that she is slipping out of her clothes.

Oh, God. I just had a horrible thought! You don't know anyone in China, do you?

Checking my email again!

Boy. How late do you usually sleep?

If you will get out of bed, we can go have your REWARD breakfast right now, if you will just *get up* and go on Craigslist. *Get up get up get up.*

Please don't call China. You better not have called China. If I have to end up paying for calls to China and/or any other far-off lands, your reward will reflect it, and I'm only being honest. Fair is fair.

ALL RIGHT. Fine. How about a REWARD BREAKFAST and *one* call to China. A short call. I will do a small call, a brief call, a "Hello, Ma, I am calling you on a stolen phone. I know, I laughed, too!" Okay, I'm sorry, *sorry,* not a "stolen" phone, let's say a "phone that does not belong to me and instead of flipping through the contacts list and hitting the entry that said 'home' I called China instead" phone. How about that?

Are you awake?

You're awake, aren't you? You know, I get the feeling that maybe you really are already awake and, instead of spending efforts to find the listing for a lost iPhone on Craigslist, you just might be laughing with your ma about my unhealthy relationship with my dog, not to mention the abundance of pictures of food, and sometimes alcoholic beverages. And about the Russian dancers and the slugs having sex on my patio.

The Russian dancer is not a Cossack or Tevye from *Fiddler on the Roof*. He is my husband. It was very cold that day, so he bundled up. And wore the Diplomat, a style of hat he has. Left over from when he was Hamid Karzai for Halloween. It is quite fetching on him. Anyway, to cheer me up, he did a couple of Russian dance moves one day and then fell over, evidenced by the photos on my iPhone and the blurry image of an ass, but with a belt. My husband always wears a belt. And, yes, you were right, those were slugs having coitus on my patio. I had only seen that once before, and, again, I cite proof. You should really laugh at those photos. I did. It took them *forever*.

Dude, GET OUT OF BED.

Please get out of bed.

Why won't you get out of bed?

Never mind. I already know.

You're not going to give me my phone, are you? You're going to keep it, aren't you, or sell it on eBay, or take it to some pawnshop across the river, and there are a ton of pawnshops across the river. You know I'll never find my iPhone. For the next month I'm going to stare at everyone I see talking on a phone to see if it's you, talking on my iPhone. At Safeway, at the mall, at every restaurant, everywhere I go, I'll be looking. But I'll never know for sure what you did with it, why you simply couldn't give it back, or why you thought you deserved to keep it.

You suck.

You're an asshole, and I know it's just a phone, but, really, what did you think when you found it? Could you have possibly thought that someone abandoned it on purpose, maybe someone who was too young to handle the responsibility of the iPhone and thought that by leaving it in a wet, shiny place with lots of traffic that it might have a better chance at life with a different family? If I wanted to abandon my iPhone, I would have left it in a safe place. Like a fire station.

It's not your iPhone.

It's not your iPhone.

I'm still paying for it as I write this to you.

You know, my dog is holding my Visa bill between her paws at this very moment, and I want to take a picture of it and make a joke about her reading the fine print and saying, "You know, if you pay this one day late . . ." but I CAN'T.

I'm going back to using a Sharpie to scrawl "This was stolen from Laurie Notaro" on everything I own.

You better not have called China.

But if you did, guess what?

Your ma is going to get another phone call, one from me, on my new iPhone. And I'm going to tell her everything.

Sincerely,
Laurie Notaro

P.S. I hope I see you sitting on a curb one day while someone is breaking your heart.

Forecasting World Destruction

❧

"Did you get Mom's email?" my sister asked me the moment I picked up the phone. "Because this is a good one. All I'm going to say is: Beware of anyone named Karen. They are bad, bad people. You know a Karen, don't you? Wasn't she one of your bridesmaids? Well, I'd sever those ties if I were you, or you'll live to regret it."

"Oh, I'm sure," I agreed. "An email from Mom is a lesson in terror."

My mother chose to prepare all three of her girls for a life outside the nest by scaring the shit out of us at every opportunity. For other little children, a visit to the grocery store might have just been a boring trip to pick up ingredients for dinner, but for the Notaro girls, it was an exercise in human nature.

In the produce department, it might have looked like we were picking out a head of lettuce, but my mother was actually homeschooling us in the subject of "Don't Be a Tramp" when she looked at the woman sorting through the green beans two feet away, whose halter top wasn't keeping all that it should under wraps.

"Lentils stay covered," my mother warned us under her

breath. "When even a little pops out, that's the same thing as being naked. And what is being naked?"

"Dirty," we all replied.

"And that means you're not normal," my mother added, tossing a head of iceberg into the cart. "And now I can't buy green beans. She touched every single one with those hands."

In the candy aisle, we passed by a friend of mine from school, who had a permanent rumbling cough, and her mother, who was wearing a housecoat and had her hair in curlers.

We exchanged smiles and I waved quickly.

"Don't you dare ever go to that girl's house and put your mouth on anything, and I mean a glass, a soda can, or a Popsicle," my mother warned me. "Why do you think she has a cough like that?"

"They're dirty?" we all replied.

"No!" my mother shot back. "They're *filthy*! I can't imagine what the inside of that house looks like. I heard that they have *cats*. God. I don't know why we can't smoke in here."

On the way out to the parking lot, my mother pointed to an Econoline three spaces away from our station wagon.

"Don't ever walk next to a van, unless being kidnapped is your goal for the day," she said, as she dragged my sister by her arm beyond a fifteen-foot radius of the vehicle. "Only weirdos drive vans. It's not normal.

"See that door?" she continued, pointing to the large sliding panel on the side of the van as she loaded the groceries into our car. "Takes two seconds to slide that thing open, grab you, and slide it back. No one would see a thing. You wanna be kidnapped, take your time walking past it. You wanna stay alive, you better friggin' *run*."

I took my mother's advice to heart. To this day, I don't even drink out of the same glass as my husband, and he will be the first to admit that he couldn't pick my cleavage, if it does indeed exist, out of a boobie lineup. Additionally, as a result of my mother's parenting, I spent my formative years sprinting past any van I saw in a parking lot like lions were chasing me, fueled by my mother's warning that eventually, someday, if I didn't pick up the pace and remained the slowest girl in any parking lot, tragedy would befall me and I'd end up begging for change, wearing a sister-wife dress of calico, somewhere in Utah. When I was twenty, however, she upped the ante and amended the warning to include the fact that Van People were now working in tandem, or as independent contractors, and that I should circumvent any two large vehicles parked next to each other or with an empty spot in between.

"Two against one," she warned. "And they don't care how stupid your hair looks dyed that way. I wouldn't kidnap you, but Van People aren't very picky."

Those words haunted me. To this day, if the only parking spot left in the grocery store is between two vans, chances are we'll be having Pizza Hut for dinner and I'll just come back the next day to get the milk.

Now, in my mother's defense, she is the cleanest person I know and kept an absolutely spotless house, so everyone is dirty to her. I've seen her look at the baseboards in hospitals and cringe in disgust. During my entire childhood, I never once saw a speck of dust on anything or so much as a crumb on the floor, a streak on the window or on the floor-to-ceiling mirrors we had in the hall. I, unfortunately, did not get the green light on that chromosome and received the signal for toe hair instead.

She also grew up in Brooklyn and saw weird people doing weird things every day, and by the time we left in the 1970s, New York's weirdness was at a fever pitch; I'm sure that left an imprint on her somewhere. This is just a theory that has taken me the better part of a lifetime to form, but I believe it. My mother believes in "normal." But my mother is also a no-nonsense sort of person, and when she identifies whatever it is she considers dangerous, or "abnormal," she reacts swiftly and without hesitation to cut it off at the source.

For example, yesterday my five-year-old nephew saw a pregnant lady and asked my very unprepared sister, the same one who was willing to wander into the fifteen-foot snatching radius of the van, "Where does the baby come out?"

"At the hospital" was my mother's response, without so much as a second's pause.

This is not to say that she is a master of strategy, because there are times when her instincts have led her astray. Some impulses aren't always positive—as in having an argument with your fourteen-year-old daughter about setting the table one night and then spreading that dirty laundry to a priest. The next thing you know, you've booked the both of you for a mother–daughter weekend retreat at your church to repair the fractured relationship caused by your rebellious and unruly teen.

Now, while I don't think I was tricked into going, I'm pretty sure I never agreed to spending two days with my mother in a nun's room and eating the cuisine of the food bank. I *know* I wouldn't have agreed to canned green beans at five meals out of six. But at fourteen, if your parents say, "You're going to spend the weekend at church with your mother to learn how to be a normal teenager," you go. There was no choice to be had. My mother, however, was pretty excited about the retreat; she expected to immediately get down to business and solve the problem of my unruliness now that I was wearing a bra and had an onslaught of hormones comparable to angry Mongols surging through my body.

Once she explained our problems to the priest—my uncleanliness, my snotty attitude, and the fact that I was still not running fast enough by vans (clear indications that I was destined for a life of abnormality and certain dust)—everyone at Bad Daughter Camp was bound to bestow upon her unparalleled amounts of sympathy and, if conditions were right, pity. She knew this. She was ready for it. She expected nothing less.

An hour after we checked in and dragged our suitcases to the nun's block, we found ourselves sitting on metal folding chairs in a half circle in "group." While she didn't show it, I imagine it was a bit of a surprise to my mom, who was sitting next to me, that every other girl enrolled in Bad Daughter Camp was either dabbling in heroin, a runaway who had lived in a tunnel, had stabbed someone with a mechanical pencil during a robbery at Circle K, or was forced to attend by the conditions of their release from juvenile detention, according to their "testimony" as we each took turns telling our "Harried Mother/Bad Daughter Tale of Woe."

When our turn came, things might have ended differently had we been given warning or even a syllabus. We might have been able to huddle and been more prepared, but we were nothing short of a disaster. I don't know about my mother, but I certainly felt the energy of the room drop and disappointment abound when she dramatically confessed that, instead of truly cleaning my room, including the baseboards, I just shoved everything in a closet or under my bed and "that wasn't normal." I do believe the other mothers actively rolled their eyes, and one crossed her arms in defiance. Even the mention that my mother had attended the notorious high school depicted in *Welcome Back, Kotter* didn't earn us any street cred. My mother tried to bring it back by suggesting that I may have smoked on one suspicious occasion or that I purchased a Devo album with my babysitting money, but by then it was too late. Our only hope for redemption was if she had suddenly gone for the gold and inserted the word "pimp" into our sordid tale of nothing, but in the presence of a priest, the consequences were too vast, although even he looked bored. Sure, I would have been a firecracker at band camp, but at Bad Daughter Camp turned into Felony Camp, I couldn't even catch a spark. I found myself almost wishing I had taken a shard of glass to someone's kidney or had set fire to something flammable, even just to my Kmart monkey pajamas, so I would have fit in and had something to talk about with the other girls on break instead of "Yeah . . . I talk back. I've done it several times now."

To add insult to injury, Felony Camp also called for us to hug after every "breakthrough," which to other mother–daughter duos meant a concession to try methadone (although the decision about cocaine was still iffy); a compromise to take the alarm off the window if the daughter would stop crawling through it; a deal to meet with another's parole officer when she was scheduled if her boyfriend was allowed to stay the night. But for my mother and me, progress was measured in reckless promises to hang up the towel instead of throwing it on the floor after a shower or to stop listening to "Whip It" so loud in my room. If there was an option of skipping the "Hug Bug," we would have certainly chosen it and volunteered to spend the weekend opening cans of greens beans manually instead.

But that option wasn't offered, and the first time we were forced to embrace was awkward at best. It was like trying to push two magnets together, each repelled by the force of the other. It would have been merciful if someone had stepped in to stop the carnage, but no one did, and the attempt continued with the approach of different angles and loss of eye contact, until we accidentally touched chins in the agonizing dance of trying to entwine and avoid each other and we both simultaneously called that contact.

We're simply not a huggy/touchy family, we're just not. Previous to the chin brush, I don't believe my mother and I had had any deliberate touching since I was about seven, and even up to that point it was merely concerning the matter of tying my shoes or washing my hair. If you wanted a hug, that's what stuffed animals and kindergarten teachers were for. My mother had dusting, vacuuming, and mopping to do. Life wasn't one big lovefest, is what I think she was trying to tell us, and the sooner you figured that out, the better off you were. Wanna be hugged a lot? Walk slow past vans.

I've never asked my mother why we were not a hugging family, because I already knew the answer. "Well, did you want to be hugged or did you want to live?" she would have said. "I could have spent my time hugging you or I could have spent my time telling you not to touch hot stoves or take candy from men. Which did you want?"

To my mother's great distress, we left Felony Camp as the most unpopular people, both our heads hanging low, neither of us being the fractured badasses she believed us to be.

"None," my mother pointed out as we waited for my dad and sisters to pick us up, "of those people in there are normal. And I'm betting you if your daughter lives in a tunnel, your house is probably filthy and your floor hasn't been waxed in years."

Recognizing a foul move when she saw it, my mother never tried to enroll me in another behavior-modification camp, nor did we ever again intrude within two feet of each other's personal space, lest our chins accidentally graze.

But that never meant that she was done throwing thoughts

of perennial terrors at me or my sisters; quite to the contrary. It was my mother's job to steel us against harmful influences in the world; it was essential that we knew that not everyone had good intentions and that immediate trust was for people who did not grow up in New York City. If someone was nice to you for no reason, they were lying and they wanted something from you; if someone asked you for directions, they really wanted to steal your kidney; if you gave a hobo a dollar, they were going to spend it on something illegal, although to be truthful, I have failed my mother horribly in that subject. In full disclosure, I have a regular hobo that I sometimes subsidize on a corner not far from my house. He's got one eye that looks at you and another eye that rolls around like a marble in an empty mayonnaise jar, so, really, I don't care if he takes the two bucks I just handed him and he puts it toward a pint of the cheapest vodka made on Earth. If I had a roller in my eye socket, I'd want to catch a buzz, and if some stupid lady in a Prius handed me her spare change and said, "Now, don't get drunk with this!" I can tell you that the stink eye shooting in her direction would be revolving at a full 360 degrees.

But if my mother saw that, she would say that's a lesson I would most likely learn the hard way when the hobo followed me home and robbed me of everything valuable on the left side of my house, but I live several states away and she hasn't made any plans to visit. That, however, has not hampered her need to cultivate her perennial terror output, which certainly was the case when she got email and some unnamed person—who would someday pay the price by being unprepared to answer sex-ed questions from her five-year-old—taught her where the "send" button was.

Since the advent of the combination of letters "FWD," my mother has resurrected her quest to expose all hidden dangers in the world, large and small, lest they pop up at some unexpected time in the form of perhaps a cellphone charger and expose themselves as the instruments of death that they are.

Or, for that matter, as people named Karen.

So when my sister called me to warn of the dangers that lie within Women Named Karen, it was clear my mother had a direct connection to it.

And there it was when I checked my email: "FWD: FWD: FWD: FWD: FWD: PLEASE READ," which in email code means "Forecasting World Destruction," and the more times it's repeated in the subject, the more times the world has the potential to be destroyed. It was a signal from my mother, flashing like a beacon in the middle of a dangerous and about to be decimated world sea.

Although my mother has never sent her kids any tips on life's essentials, such as "There's a thing called an egg and a sperm," "Make sure to drink lots of milk to prevent bone loss," "Boobs or kids: Pick one and go with it, because you can't have both," or "It's too bad that you went to the doctor to see if you were turning albino, because we go gray everywhere, especially in parts where your colorist charges extra," her call to nurture has never deviated from its chosen path.

As I soon as I opened the email, I was warned, "We received a call last week from the 809 area code. The woman left a message that said, 'Hey, this is Karen. Sorry I missed you—get back to me quickly. I have something important to tell you.' Then she repeated a phone number beginning with 809. We did not respond."

To set the record straight, my mother did not receive a call from Karen, nor did anyone she knows, but whoever Karen called originally in 1998 typed up this Forecasting World Destruction email and sent it out into the abyss. It then took an

Oregon Trail's worth of wormholes and then a hop on string theory during its path of destiny to finally reach my mother, who then found it terrifying enough to spread even further after reading the first use of the word coupling "DO NOT," which began the email.

Now, it turns out that if you were curious enough to call Karen back, you'd just opened up a world of hurt for yourself, which never would have happened if you had a mother like mine. Because if your mother had valued Karen's phone call far and above, say, "No one ever tells you this, but when you turn forty, your uterus will stage a coup that you can only fight with Vicodin, so ask your doctor for it NOW," you would have already known that Karen's area code—"809, 284, AND 876"—is located in the Dominican Republic. Even if you just call and say, "Hi, Karen, this is Carol Notaro, and I know you don't have an important message for me but I put you on my prayer chain anyway!" you will apparently be charged $2,425 per minute.

YES, YOU WILL, because *your* careless mother neglected to tell you that your local phone company will not get involved and will tell you that they are simply providing the billing, and, just like that, you are out $2,425 per minute. Isn't that scary? Wouldn't you trade a hug to have the equivalent of your mortgage payment back? Apparently fifteen people on my mother's email "CC: Ponzi scheme" thought it was frightening enough to keep passing it on like an open herpes sore until it finally got to me. In fact, it is so alarming that the email itself pleads for the reader to send it on.

I mean, how many times have people teetered on the precipice of calling 809? Countless. *Countless.* In fact, there are people who have to stop themselves from doing it right now. And if you loved someone, you would have the same response my mother did ("Oh! That's terrible! Animals!") and immediately click the Forecasting World Destruction button, as soon as you added the names of everyone you play bingo with, go to church with, or have ever asked for a casserole recipe. Of course it seems odd that Karen coincidentally only seems to call when she knows no one will answer and then slips back into the inky, evil shadows of the Dominican Republic Area Code Scam, but that's how those people work! Who is Karen, the answer begs? Does she know when you are sleeping? Does she know when you're awake? Does she know if you've been bad or good, so be good for goodness' sake?

And if that wasn't terrifying enough, another ball of fright was headed my way when my mother sent me the "FWD: FWD: FWD: FWD: FWD: MAKE SURE YOUR DAUGHTERS KNOW! & EVERYONE ELSE" email, which included a note that "This was written by a guy from KVLY-TV in Fargo. This is true. Scary!"

Because if that confirmation doesn't ink this stamp of Bill O'Reilly's approval, I don't know what would.

It turns out that people at truck stops and Walmarts will follow you and ask you what kind of perfume you are wearing, then offer you that very perfume at a bargain-basement price. According to the Guy From KVLY-TV in Fargo, the men will stand between parked cars and ask you to sniff the perfume they are selling, and if you haven't already sensed the danger of a man standing between parked cars (must share a common ancestor with the Van People), when you sniff the perfume, you'll pass out.

BECAUSE IT IS ETHER! And then you will be pickpocketed as you lie helpless on the asphalt of a discount retailer, and hopefully your fall will be strategic enough that you'll miss both the puddle of Bud Light upchuck and the dirty diaper from the baby whose parents are trying to sell her by the entrance.

According to email legend, this has happened in the parking lots of Big Lots, as well, and although I'm not going to comment about why I'm not sure thinning the herd is all that bad of an idea, I will say that, if there are people game for the sniff test moments before spending six bucks on sweatpants at Walmart, there is an audience for this, if anyone can capture it on film. Not to mention that if any of these centers of commerce are regular destinations—not ones visited under duress or during a kidnapping scenario—whatever scent you throw on your body bears the notes of embalming fluid or gasoline, anyway, and if spending a dollar less on it in a parking lot from a guy who has missing teeth and facial scabs is even remotely a good idea to you, then you deserve to land in that diaper and have your wallet plundered for the six dollars plus change that was in it.

Then, almost as if my mother got them in a "Violence Against Women" bundle, like independent film stations on cable, four came in quick succession like a meteor shower:

1. "*FWD: FWD: FWD: FWD: Must know about*77*" (I think this one originated at the same moment hominids split off from apes, because it took me two minutes to scroll past all the "FWD"s):

   I knew about the red light on cars, but not the *77. It was about 1:00 P.M. in the afternoon, and Lauren was driving to visit a friend. An UNMARKED police car pulled up behind her and put his lights on. Lauren dialed *77 and the police came immediately. The police pulled the guy from the car and tackled him to the ground. The man was a convicted rapist and wanted for other crimes, including previous Impersonating an Officer charges.

2. *"FWD: FWD: FWD: DO NOT open the door for a crying baby"*:

Someone just told me that her friend heard a crying baby on her porch the night before last, and she called the police because it was late and she thought it was weird. The police told her "Whatever you do, DO NOT open the door."

The lady then said that it sounded like the baby had crawled near a window, and she was worried that it would crawl to the street and get run over. The policeman told her that they think a serial killer has a baby's cry recorded and uses it to coax women out of their homes thinking that someone dropped off a baby.

3. *"FWD: Read—important"*:

THE RECENT TRAGEDY OF A YOUNG WOMAN BEING KID-NAPPED AND EVENTUALLY KILLED, AFTER SHE HAD REPEAT-EDLY GIVEN THE KIDNAPPER A WRONG PIN TO HER ATM CARD. IF SHE KNEW THE METHOD BELOW, SHE COULD HAVE BEEN SAVED. SO I THINK IT IS IMPORTANT ENOUGH TO LET YOU KNOW.

IF YOU SHOULD EVER BE FORCED BY A ROBBER TO WITH-DRAW MONEY FROM AN ATM MACHINE, YOU CAN NOTIFY THE POLICE BY ENTERING YOUR PIN # IN REVERSE. FOR EXAMPLE, IF YOUR PIN NUMBER IS 1234, THEN YOU WOULD PUT IN 4321. THIS INFORMATION WAS RECENTLY BROAD-CASTED ON FOX TV.

4. *"FWD: FWD: FWD: FWD: FWD: NOT TEA PARTY RE-LATED"* (I swear I am not making that title up):

The first thing men look for in a potential victim is hairstyle. They are most likely to go after a woman with a ponytail, bun, braid or other hairstyle that can easily be grabbed. They are also likely to go after a woman with long hair. Women with short hair are not common targets. Men are most likely to attack & rape in the early morning, between 5:00a.m. and 8:30a.m., and will not rape women carrying umbrellas.

The time had come. Even though I had replied to my mother after each and every Forecasting World Destruction bulletin, telling her they were all hoaxes, she kept sending them, one after another. Finally, I felt I had no choice but to call her.

"Mom," I began. "Thank you for sending me the emails to remind me of all the grisly ways I could potentially die."

"No problem," she said simply. "That's my job."

"Well," I said hesitantly, "I think that it's great that now we all know how to punch out the taillights of cars and wave our hands through the hole while we're being held hostage in the trunk of a car by a man who plans to use our skulls as soup bowls, but the emails you are sending us aren't true."

"What do you mean? Of course they're true," my mother insisted. "They wouldn't be able to send them around if they weren't true."

"Mom, remember when I was in my twenties and there was a time period of about four to six, possibly seven, years when you were very mad that I didn't have a job?" I asked.

"Oh," my mother replied with a laugh. "Are you trying to suggest that you have a job now?"

"Well," I said, trying to ignore her, "what I was doing during the day was going to college in journalism school. And what I learned in journalism school was basically to check stuff out. And now *you* can do that, too. I've sent you a couple of replies that have a link in them to a website that can tell you if something you get in an email is true or if it's an urban legend."

There was silence on the other end of the line.

"The emails I sent you about the website snopes.com?" I asked. "Did you get them?"

"I don't know," my mother finally answered. "Maybe I did."

"How do you not know if you got them or not?" I asked suspiciously.

"I may have deleted some of them," she said.

"Some of them?" I asked.

"Well, most of them, really," she answered. "Actually, all of them. When your name pops up in the list, I just hit 'delete.'"

"You don't even open them?" I asked, a little stunned.

"Most of what you say is nonsense," she informed me.

"Oh," I said, nodding my head. "It's nonsense? You think it's nonsense? Of course, hitting *77 is nothing short of scientific theory, because guess what? Not only is dialing *77 only useful in a handful of counties in the United States, but it's the exact number of keys required to hit 911, which works . . . well, *everywhere*."

"They couldn't send out the email if it wasn't true," my mother insisted. "When I get pulled over by an unmarked police car driven by a serial killer, I am dialing *77!"

"Okay, fine," I snipped. "Push *77. You go right ahead. And when your abductor takes you to the ATM at gunpoint, you try to remember your birthday backward, but don't worry, because you have plenty of time. The police will never come, because there is no backward-pin-number panic signal. It doesn't exist; it's an urban legend. And guess what I'm going to do right now? I'm going to go to the closest Walmart and ask anyone walking by if they'll sell me cheap perfume, but only if they can test some on me with a squirt bottle! In my face! In my face!"

"You'd better not!" my mother warned. "It's *ether*, Laurie! It says it in the email! *It's not perfume!*"

"I'm putting my hair in a ponytail!" I threatened.

"Go ahead and be an idiot!" my mother countered. "It's like putting a handle on your head. Try to grab a pitcher without a handle. It's almost impossible!"

"I have to go now, Mom!" I said, my voice rising. "I hear a crying baby on my porch and I'm afraid it's going to crawl into traffic! Bye! Bye! If you hear me scream, please push *LIES!"

I didn't hear from my mom for a while after that, which was probably for the best, especially since I was still making a point of not carrying an umbrella until after 9:30 A.M. But then one day it came, a message too important to ignore, an email too frightening to deny. Doing what all good mothers do; trying to ensure my survivability.

"FWD: FWD: FWD: verry important to know!"

And there, unfolding before me in red 70-point Helvetica:

A few days ago, a person was recharging his mobile phone at home. Just at that time a call came in and he answered it with the charger still connected to the outlet.

After a few seconds electricity flowed into the cell phone unrestrained and the young man was thrown to the floor with a heavy thud. As you can see, the phone actually exploded. [Inserted here is a photo of a charred, dirty mattress that has clearly been on fire.]

His parents rushed to the room only to find him unconscious, with a weak heartbeat and burnt fingers.

He was rushed to the nearby hospital, but was pronounced dead on arrival.

[Inserted here is a photo of the dead man's hand, cooked, with fingers swollen to the size of Ball Park franks. They plump when you cook them.]

Cell phones are a very useful modern invention.

However, we must be aware that it can also be an instrument of death.

Never use the cell phone while it is hooked to the electrical outlet! If you are charging the cell phone and a call comes in, unplug it from the charger and outlet.

FORWARD THIS TO THE PEOPLE THAT MATTER IN YOUR LIFE!!!

Clearly, in the world of FWD, this was a hallmark moment. Never before had my mother sent an email that was illustrated with photos featuring the hands of the corpse. I mean, really, it was almost proof. For a moment I was lost in the excitement of the bloated, waxy sausage fingers, and I thought, I can't believe I've answered an instrument of death when it was being charged and I lived! I am still alive!!

And then, as if there was a cherry on this cake, I spotted something incredible in the very last line: "Verified by snopes.com!," followed by a link.

Wow. I thought, I am impressed. Finally, my mother has sent me a true Forecast of World Destruction. I couldn't believe it. The fear was real. It was justified! In fact, I had just gotten up to unplug my instrument of death when I sat back down and decided to click the link.

And, to be honest, much to my dismay, the page that came

up was indeed to snopes.com but was a blank page that said only, "You wanted *what?*"

A dead link. No such page.

I took a deep breath and reached for the phone, since I was positive my mother was about to embark on a door-to-door mission to inform her neighbors of the catastrophe, armed with the "dead hands" photo as evidence. To her, sending the email with photographic evidence that the fear was real was not only an accomplishment, but a message to me that every time she had sent out another FWD, she really was helping to stop someone from dialing a truly evil area code or being roasted by a cellphone charger or keeping a serial killer who was terrified of umbrellas from impersonating an officer.

I dialed the right area code for her phone number (the temptation to dial 809 still soooo great) and then stopped.

I looked at the last line of the email again.

"FORWARD THIS TO THE PEOPLE THAT MATTER IN YOUR LIFE!!!"

I thought for a minute.

And with that, I hung up the phone.

The Burn Test

The first time I walked into the kitchen of the house I would eventually buy, the current owner saw my eyes immediately catch fire when they saw the stove. It was a huge late-forties white enameled antique gas stove with cast-iron burners and big, rounded corners, and it was the finest piece of stove porn I had ever seen in my life. I do recall actually having to catch my breath. It was so big it gobbled up six inches of the doorway, and rightfully so. Despite the fact that I was ready to make her an offer based on the white giant in the kitchen, the woman noticed my leer and quickly stepped in front of the stove, as if to protect her young from a predator. She wasted no time in telling me that the stove was not staying; it had been her grandmother's and was coming with her to the new house.

"We have a stove in the basement that we'll replace it with," she added. "It's a KitchenAid."

Which was a drag, since I had left a similar yet not nearly as grand stove behind in our last house, and felt compelled to do so because it was original to the bungalow I'd just sold. It would have been greedy to break them up.

Indeed, true to their word, the former owners had the

KitchenAid in place when we moved in, although they neglected to mention that I'd run three cars into the ground since that thing was considered "new."

Getting the KitchenAid stove to even function was a process. Before the burners would consider glowing red, there was a series of bumps, groans, and moans that sounded like it was listing and in comparison made the *Titanic* seem silent when sinking, prompting us to change its name to First Aid. I didn't even get what was *in* the stove that was making those sounds, unless it was a portal to hell and we were roasting souls every time we made macaroni and cheese.

I had no idea that I hated the First Aid as much as I did; it was just a stove, it served its purpose, I suppose, as long as I considered that only cooking over a hearth in my kitchen with kindling could take longer to get a heat element working. But one day I looked at it and it made me mad and I decided that I hated its stupid glowy burners, its almond color, and the arthritis it apparently had. I remembered, in pristine detail, how great the old stove looked in this kitchen, and I also missed the gas stove I'd left behind.

I immediately went to eBay, typed "old stove" in the search box, and, within seconds, there it was: a gorgeous old O'Keefe & Merritt, the Cadillac of antique stoves, for sale, fifty miles away in Salem.

The woman who was selling it seemed very nice and within an hour emailed that I should meet her at her storage unit. I asked my husband to come along, just in case I was never heard from again and my mummy was found a decade later in various Rubbermaid totes after an auction of the contents of #209 at Hoarder Storage in Salem, Oregon.

"Yeah," he agreed. "I don't think they could fit you into just one."

"Did you know," I casually mentioned, "that when the wife suddenly vanishes, it's usually because the husband rented a wood chipper?"

"I wouldn't even know how to turn one on," he replied. "Everyone would know that. I've broken everything with an 'on' button even remotely related to household maintenance."

"Okay, then you have fun sharing an eight-by-eight with your cellie, George the Whore, for the next ten years until they find my head in a cake carrier," I added.

"I've heard Salem has some of the most beautiful storage-unit structures in the state," he said wearily. "Meet you at the car."

It became clear that my fear of being dismembered was rather empty when we spotted the stove lady, Tina, at the entrance with her twelve-year-old son. She was very nice and friendly, but we hadn't been in the elevator for half a minute when Tina confessed that she loved the stove and really didn't want to part with it yet had to out of necessity. I nodded and smiled, knowing a sales ploy when I saw one. The soft pitch.

"There's a man who's interested in coming to see it tomorrow," she added, putting a little bit of arm into the second ball.

Sure there is, I thought, as I smiled and nodded at her again. The elevator doors opened and we followed her down the hall to her unit. My husband and I stood back as she raised the unit door, and I braced myself for disappointment after seeing her dilapidated stove, which probably had rodents nesting in it. Yes, the photos on eBay were beautiful, but when I take a picture of myself from a higher angle, I shave off two chins, control my nose hair, and shrink the girth of my nostrils faster than a surgeon with a beach house in Malibu who texts when he drives. Tricks of the trade, my friend.

As the door rolled up, it revealed a hulking shape with a

tarp draped over it. I held my breath, and as her son pulled the tarp off, I gasped. A harp strummed somewhere, and a chorus of angels sang that one note that they do when something incredible happens and changes everything forever.

It did not look like the stove in the eBay photo; it looked better. It looked incredible. There was a chrome griddle in the center, a periscope window on the backsplash to see down into the oven without opening the door, a Grillevator, a warming oven, and it was all in absolutely pristine condition for a stove that came off the assembly line in 1954. When I opened the oven door, it was so clean it was almost impossible to believe that anyone had ever cooked in it. The chrome on it gleamed, the white enamel shone, and I swear the corners of the oven doors curled up and smiled at me.

"I really don't want to sell it, but I have to," Tina repeated. "We sold the piano last week. This is the last thing I have left from the house I had with my husband. He was killed by a drunk driver on New Year's Day several years ago, and this is like saying a final goodbye."

And then she looked at me and started to cry.

Oh boy.

"I'm sorry," I said, as her son hugged her and they both relived the pain of that New Year's Day. She patted his head. And then he began to sob, too.

"We moved up here because my husband's brother said he would be a father figure to my sons," she continued, as tears streamed down her face. "But that didn't happen. It turns out he's . . . he's not the man we thought he was."

Oh, Jesus, I said to myself, as I released the grip on my wallet. I thought the worst thing that could happen at the storage unit was that I'd be lured into a trap, lose my life in a valiant struggle, get divvied up like a chicken, and be left to rot in the dark, but a weeping widow clutching her fatherless son as they remembered the fun family stove time was a little bit beyond my established skill set.

And that's when I looked at my husband, and it looked like he super wanted to punch me in the face with that stove.

"I'm going to cook on it a lot," I mouthed to him.

As far as Tina & Son were concerned, I didn't know what to do. If it was an act, it was a good one; it had the same amounts of embarrassment, despair, agony, and vulnerability as Courtney Love's *Behind the Music* episode. But it seemed real to me, and honestly, if this was a ploy, wouldn't there be easier things to sell than old appliances? It's not like there's a band of antique stove bandits who will wait until you go on vacation to bust down your door to steal an heirloom that requires a dolly, a ramp, and a can of Easy-Off.

So, believing that what I was seeing was true, and despite the fact that I am an inappropriate hugger who has trouble assessing when the time is right, I kind of reached out and tried to comfort this person—whom I had only known since the storage-place front door—and I wasn't sure what my hand was going to do once it made a landing. At the last second, my palm sort of curled up like a claw, and then I found I was rubbing the back of my pointer finger up and down a square-inch area of her arm three times, albeit awkwardly. That really was as much as I could do, given the prep time, atmosphere, and the fact that I was getting kind of hungry.

To jolt us back into the reality of why I drove fifty miles and dragged my husband—who was now wishing he knew how to turn on a wood chipper—with me, I spoke to Tina quietly but very, very compassionately, and I mean so compassionately it was almost a whisper, it was gentle, very soft, like baby talk. Like tiny, little—like I was breathing it but with light, airy words.

"So in the email you said you'd take three seventy-five," I whispered, but unfortunately, after all of that, it really did come out more like a regular old everyday whisper, like something you'd whisper to someone who probably wasn't crying and clinging to their son but who had their foot on the back of your seat in a movie theater.

Tina wiped the tears away and raised her head. "The guy that was coming tomorrow was going to offer me five hundred dollars," she informed me.

"Five hundred?" I asked, somewhat surprised, and not in a whisper. "Okay, five? We can do five; consider it part of the pain and suffering, sure. Five. We can do five. Five is awesome. It's awesome."

And then I quickly counted out the $375 in cash I had brought and wrote a check for the remaining amount.

So while I don't want to say that I swindled a widow out of an incredible stove, I am pretty sure I swindled a widow out of an incredible stove, even if she upped the ante on that last hand. When I went home that night and did some research, I saw that the same model that was sitting under a tarp in a storage place was selling regularly for considerably more, so I didn't exactly feel that my compassionate finger touch was for nothing. The stove was in my kitchen by the weekend, and I cooked pancakes on the chrome griddle that following Sunday.

There was only one thing missing on the new old stove, and that was a working timer. It was completely forgivable and easily remedied; I went straight back to eBay, my reliable source for everyone else's trash, and looked for a vintage one that matched the era of the stove.

I found several that fit the bill right away, marked one to watch, to see how high the bidding went. And, at the last second, I was outbid on the vintage Lux Presto timer in chrome. I moved on to my next-favorite timer, an old Mirro aluminum one, watched it, bid on it, and was outbid. And outbid again on the aqua Minute Minder.

Now, I have to say here that I am not an eBay novice. I found my stove on it, for shit's sake. I know how it works, and I typically, with exceptions here and there, walk away with what I want for a fair-to-bargain price. But I was getting outfoxed every single time I bid on an old, perfect timer, and it was starting to make me mad. After losing three of them, it dawned on me that the winning bidder's user name was becoming a little familiar.

As I went down the list of timers I'd lost, I thought it was odd that KOOKAROO, who outbid me at the last second on the Presto, was the same one who outbid me on the Mirro. The intrigue became deeper as I realized the winner was the same for the aqua Minute Minder, too.

What do you need with three old timers? I thought. How many stoves can one person have? How many pans of brownies is he making? Curious to see if KOOKAROO simply had the same taste that I did or if he was stalking me—because, after all, I was basically stalking him—I clicked on his profile, and that's when I saw something weird.

KOOKAROO hadn't bought just the three timers that I wanted. He had bought all kinds of timers—vintage timers, plastic timers, egg-shaped timers, and darkroom timers—and then had them shipped to Germany, where he apparently lived. One hundred fifty of them, and that was only what was listed on his feedback, which most likely was a slim margin of how many auctions he had actually won. He had not purchased one single thing aside from kitchen timers, and the 150 he had collected were in the past two weeks alone. That's more than ten times a day. That's a lot of brownies.

I wasn't the only one who thought it was odd. Just to make sure it wasn't me that the scenario wasn't making sense to, I ran the facts and only the facts of the case by my best friend, Jamie, who is a scientist and approaches almost everything with the scientific method, except when it comes to picking a first husband. I told her everything about the outbidding, how many he bought, and that the guy had done this in the time span of two weeks. None of them were electric timers. All of them were manual, none of them programmable or digital.

"So what do you think about that?" I questioned. "What do you think about someone who buys that many timers in fourteen days?"

"I think he abandoned his goat herd and went to a training camp where he was told he's going to get seventy-two virgins if he blows himself up in front of a falafel stand," Jamie said simply. "Even though I bet his goats were prettier than the virgins. What do I think he's doing? He's building bombs."

I asked my friend Michell, who is a cop in Florida.

I only got to the part where I said he was living in Germany when she simply said, "Bombs."

I asked my other friend Michelle, whose husband used to be a cop in Texas.

"He's eating jalapeños on top of cream cheese right now," she informed me. "But I'm pretty sure he just said 'bombs.'"

So I called my sister to get her opinion, and she answered while she was on the elliptical at the gym, watching Tyra Banks on a wide screen.

"So what do you think?" I asked her.

"Why did you buy a stove and drag it fifty miles home if the timer didn't work?" she replied between huffs. "You should have just gone to Sears."

So with the general consensus being that I had stumbled

upon a terrorist's nest, I wasn't exactly sure what to do next. I looked up the address of Homeland Security, but I wasn't all that sure what I should do after that. Did I proceed? Did I just ignore it? Was I overreacting, or was I being naïve? Was I being Mrs. Kravitz? There was no middle ground here.

I decided the only way to know what was responsible was to make a list of pros and cons. So I did.

Pro: You could be foiling an international plot to kill innocent people. And those people might even be Americans.

Con: They're *kitchen timers*. What if someone just got an impulse to buy every kitchen timer he could possibly get his hands on or decided he wanted to break a world record and was absolutely unskilled at anything else? Sometimes people need to feel special.

Pro: That's ridiculous. Kitchen timers would be one of the last things anybody would collect. If you can blink your eyes, you can break a world record, with some self-determination and Rockstar energy drinks. Eat some beans and fart a thousand times. That's a record.

Con: That's precisely why kitchen timers are an excellent choice. They are unexpected. They are free-spirited and out of the ordinary. Just because they don't fit into your box. Follow your bliss!

Pro: How would you feel if you ignored this and next week a bomb went off in Germany? He's probably living in Hani Hanjour's apartment!

Con: I would have no idea if it was KOOKAROO who used the kitchen timers to set off bombs. Everyone should be homeschooled!

Pro: You could help capture a dangerous person who is probably on welfare and using my tax money to buy RC Cola and Little Debbies. This terrorist needs to get up off his ass and get a job and stop tinkering with little timer parts! Be a productive member of society and pay taxes!

Con: You could be ruining a dork's life. I wish I could breast-feed something.

Pro: If collecting kitchen timers was a life, then being renditioned would be an upgrade. I hate you, Con.

Con: I hated you first, Pro.

Pro: You live in a trailer and you start drinking too early in the morning. Why don't you go write a letter to one of your convict boyfriends?

Con: How was your Tea Party rally? I see you have a nice little sign on the back of an old Papa John's pizza box with the word "consitution" scrawled in black marker.

Clearly, Pro and Con were no help. I abandoned that effort after Con tried to hug Pro, saying that they needed to come together and that diversity was good, and Pro responded by flipping the pizza box over to the other side and scribbling "We Came Unarmed—This Time."

I found myself wishing there was a smoking car parked at the curb or a guy looking suspicious when he asked for an extra side of tahini and a remote detonator. But all I had was a person who was buying a stupid amount of kitchen timers on an auction site, and the last thing I wanted to do was narc off some idiot who was building the world's biggest kitchen-timer robot. I decided I would write an email to Homeland Security, just to see if once I got it down in words it sounded as crazy or as serious as I thought it did.

Dear Homeland Security:

This is going to sound crazy.

I bid on a kitchen timer on eBay. A guy outbid me three times for different kitchen timers, and I clicked on his feedback to see how much he usually paid for items to judge how high of a bidder he was. On his feedback, I saw that the man buys nothing but kitchen timers. At least 150 of them since the middle of May when he joined eBay, and that's just what he has feedback on. All kinds of kitchen timers and darkroom timers. He buys nothing but timers. If anyone went into Bed Bath & Beyond and bought 150 kitchen timers in one shot, someone would think that was odd. But on eBay, he buys one at a time from different people all over the world, mostly old ones. No digital ones. Probably nothing, but I thought I should mention it.

Hopefully, he's an art student working on a kitchen-timer installation. My friend Mary suggested he was boiling thousands of eggs and was perhaps the Easter Bunny. I know that's probably not very funny. But I already feel like Lucy Ricardo even writing this email, so that's all.

Thanks,

Laurie Notaro

And then I put the email in my "saved" folder, but after writing it, I still didn't know what to do. One day I thought it was crazy, and the next I was convinced the person was a terrorist.

My husband, however, was not so unsure of what to do with the email and told me point-black that he considered the whole thing "an episode of insanity." I took his comment to heart, until I realized that we've lived in this town for years and he still doesn't know how to get to the movies and is unable to change lanes without my "help."

"I don't even remotely understand how someone who bid against you on eBay suddenly became a terrorist," he argued. "For all you know, he's building a Kitchen Timer Museum."

"A hundred and fifty timers, of all shapes and sizes, in fourteen days?" I replied. "That's a pretty hasty Kitchen Timer Museum. I wouldn't pay to see a bunch of kitchen timers slapped together. *No one would,* especially not Germans, who are masters at design!"

"I think this is all crazy talk, and I, for one, am against sending that email!" my husband informed me.

Which was fine. He was entitled his opinion; I'm cool with that. I just want to see him try to get to the 3:45 showing of the next Kate Winslet movie on his own. Especially if he has to change lanes.

I found another kitchen timer, this one a Westclox bakelite timer that was cool but looked pretty beat up, figuring that I could not only get it cheap but that there was no way any curator of the Kitchen Timer Museum would consider it for a collection. There was no way: It was missing a hand. I positioned myself at my keyboard in the last minutes of the auction; I bid; and a second before the auction ended, someone outbid me.

KOOKAROO knows no bounds, I thought, my fury building, my face flushing. KOOKAROO is selfish. I wonder if KOOKAROO ever thought for a moment that someone might not feel like eating burned chocolate chip cookies after forgetting what time she put them in the oven when she got a little carried away with some toenail cutting, and frankly, even though I understand it's a matter of perspective, burned cookies are a bigger bummer than not having the right parts for your stupid bomb.

Sorry. But that's the truth.

I hate you, KOOKAROO, I thought. I really, really hate you. Can't you even let one other person buy a timer? How many timers does it take to make a bomb, anyway? How many parts do you need? Don't you have enough for your jihad jam-boree by now? I hope every one of your virgins looks like Tori Spelling. I really, really do. You deserve that. I hope they all look like praying mantises with lopsided bocce-ball boobs and a bristly coat.

Lummox.

Oooops.

Send.

Believe it or not, I actually won a timer later that day, but to be honest, I just bid on it as a test to see if I could summon KOOKAROO and reconfirm that I had done the right thing. Even though it was only $1.79, the lesson here is that you will always pay too much for a timer shaped like a big red person-ality mushroom, "personality" meaning it has a face.

When I recounted the story later that night about why I would be getting a ticking chunk of fungus in the mail, my hus-band was not exactly happy.

"You did *what*?" he asked me, acting like I had just turned Anne Frank in. "What if the person was an art student doing a project? What if you turned in an innocent person? And did it ever dawn on you that Homeland Security knows who you are now, too?"

"You just spent the last hour making trombone sounds with your mouth, Mr. Brain," I reminded him. "And while I'm not Angela Lansbury, the pieces didn't add up. Why does anyone need that many timers? You know, it's a good thing you weren't selling hot dogs in Times Square when smoke was billowing out of that SUV or sitting next to the guy who tried to set his wiener on fire on that flight over Detroit."

"This is an *episode in insanity*!" he repeated. "They were kitchen timers! And I sounded exactly like a jazzy trombone!"

" 'See Something, Say Something!' " I yelled back. "Can we

continue this in forty-five seconds? My auction for a Glenwood chrome timer is almost up."

"You already won the Merry Mushroom timer," he reminded me. "Why do you need two? Two in one day? Who needs two timers in one day?"

"I do," I said blankly. "I'm starting the Patriot Act Timer Museum, if you must know. 'Don't Tread on My Timer.' . . . Aaaaaaaand I won! Finally! This one looks cool; it has original paint and chrome, bakelite dial. There is another one that is very Art Deco, has these great tall, skinny numbers and it's aqua, but that one doesn't end until tomorrow."

My husband nodded.

"Better be careful," he added. "You never know. I might have to say something. Because I think I just saw something."

Jenny and the French Dog

The old dog had its nose buried in the can, shoving its snout in as far as it could go to get whatever was left inside. The snow fell, gathering in a thin film on the dog's fur, then melting just as fast on the mangy, stringy coat.

"Oh, no," I said to my husband, pointing at the animal trying to fend for itself on a cold day in New York City; person after person passed by, and no one seemed to notice. Without a leash and clearly with no owner watching it, the dog made its way along the side of the building, sniffing for more food.

My husband shook his head. "I don't know what you think you can do," he said simply. "We're on vacation. It's not like you can roll a dog up in a dry-cleaning bag and put it in your suitcase. I know it's terrible to see something like that, but you're going to have to forget it. There's nothing we can do."

I realized he was right. I mean, here we were in New York, two weeks before Christmas, on a five-day trip that didn't include taking care of stray dogs. Frankly, I didn't even understand how there could be a stray dog in a city like this; did someone forget to lock the seven dead bolts on their door and the dog just wandered out? I found myself getting angry, wondering how people could be so careless. How do you lose a dog in the city?

But there it was, a large collie-shepherd mix, trying to eat rotten food out of a piece of garbage right on Bleecker Street, around the corner from the front door of the building we had rented an apartment in for our stay.

"Okay, now wait," my husband begged. "Don't get obsessive. Don't let it ruin your time here. I'm sure someone saw the dog and will call the ASPCA, they'll call the owner, and it will be back home by nightfall. Seriously. How can anyone lose a dog here?"

He was right. Someone must have realized their dog was missing and was probably looking for it right then.

"Do you really think so?" I said.

"Well, it certainly is in the realm of possibilities," he said. The traffic light turned green and he grabbed my hand and stepped off the curb, while I looked behind me at the dog taking a poop on the sidewalk and the snow falling all around it.

And we had a wonderful day; the snow eased up and we walked up and down the West Village, the East Village, stopped in for a slice of pizza, and then wandered through Washington Square Park. I bought a dress from my favorite clothes store, we stopped and had coffee at a café, and never once did I stop thinking about that old, starving dog eating out of the trash.

But much to my relief, when we got back to the apartment building, the dog was nowhere to be seen. I had images of it shivering in a corner or covered in snow, still foraging on the street, but there was no sign of it. Happily, I imagined it reunited with its owner, the both of them snuggled up in front of a warm fire, except in my honest version of the fantasy, the dog was forcing the owner to lick the remnants out of a crusty refried-beans can.

The next morning we hit Midtown, walked up Fifth Avenue to see the storefronts decorated for the holidays, then wandered around Central Park and went to the American Museum of Natural History. We returned to the apartment to get ready for dinner and were lucky enough to flag down a cab immediately after walking out of the door to the building. I got in the cab first, and when I turned to ask my husband the address of the restaurant, I gasped.

"There's the dog!" I cried, pointing.

And there, on an otherwise empty corner, not another soul around, was the shaggy dog, peeing on the sidewalk as the taxi zoomed away.

"That was the dog!" I said to my husband again. "It's lost again!"

"Either that or it never went home," my husband added. "But there's nothing we can do about it; it's kind of on its own."

I couldn't believe that dog was still out there, in the elements, lost, and no one had bothered to help it.

"Really?" I wondered aloud. "Do people just walk by and not see an old dog wandering around by itself? I can't believe it. That thing is probably starving. Order something big, because we're taking half of it back with us for the dog."

But when we returned that evening, with chops and steaks in hand, the dog, again, was gone.

It snowed again that night, and this time it snowed hard. I went downstairs twice to see if the dog was around, to give it our leftovers, but there was no sign of it or its paw prints in the snow.

The next morning, we woke up to a beautifully sunny day, although it was bitterly cold. We had brunch plans with my friend Jenny and her husband, Joe, at a café a couple of blocks down the street. The air was crisp in the way that it is only after it snows, and the minute we stepped outside I saw the dog, gingerly finding its way along the ice that had formed on the sidewalk.

I bent down.

"Don't," my husband warned. "We have to meet Jenny and Joe in fifteen minutes. What are you going to do with the dog, bring it along? There's no leash on it, Laurie. It's a stray dog. I know you feel bad, but we're a little powerless here."

Regardless, I tried calling the dog, but it wouldn't come, no matter how many times I pleaded "Here, girl!" or "Come!" or "Wanna cookie?" The dog looked at me suspiciously and then ignored me. The last thing I was going to do was try to put my hands anywhere near the dog's face to look for a collar under that matted fur, plus I knew my husband was right. The truth was that I really didn't want to call the ASPCA on the dog; it was so old and decrepit that I thought it might get put down when no one came looking for it. I knew that leaving it on the street was not good, either, but I thought the dog should have some sort of fighting chance. It was clear that it stayed in the same area, so maybe it had an urban "den" someplace close, like in *Hotel For Dogs,* which I have obviously watched too many times. I didn't know, but I was willing to stretch all limits of reason, still hopeful that whoever was looking for it would find it.

But there was no way the dog was going to come to me, and I had no idea what I would have done with it if it did. It would be one thing if we lived here, but we were leaving the day after tomorrow.

"Come on," my husband said, reaching out his hand. "I'm sorry. There's not much you can do."

So I left the dog standing in the snow as we went off to brunch, and when I looked back one last time, it was going to the bathroom by the side of the building.

Part of me said, "See? Aren't you glad you left the dog? You'd have to carry dog doo all the way to breakfast," but I couldn't help but feel like I had just done something atrocious.

We were going to be late, but I was sure that Jenny would understand. Both of her dogs came from rescue; one was blind, the other had three legs, and she had had several other dogs in the years I had known her that came from foster homes or that were difficult to place elsewhere. If there was anyone who would get it, it would be Jenny.

"I'm sorry we're late," I said as my husband and I approached Jenny and Joe, who were already seated at a table. "There is a stray dog we've been seeing on and off at the apartment building for days now. We just saw it again, but I couldn't get it to come to me."

Jenny immediately looked alarmed.

"What do you mean, 'a stray dog'?" she asked. "No one was with it? Was it running into traffic?"

"No," I said, shaking my head and sitting down. "It stays close to the building. I haven't seen it wander off the sidewalk."

"Someone will call the shelter, I'm sure of it," Joe said, trying to reassure us.

"No one's called so far, and we've seen it for three days now," I replied.

"You have got to be kidding me," Jenny gasped. "It's been snowing! It was so cold out last night! Did you feel how cold it was? Where is the building?"

"It's about three blocks from here on Bleecker," I replied.

"Oh, boy," Joe said, looking none too pleased.

"I'm not going to let a dog die of exposure, Joe," she said as she reached for her phone and started looking up phone numbers.

The waitress came over and took our order.

"We don't have time for a 'Save the Dog' mission today," he protested. "I have a list of things I need to do."

"Is letting a dog die one of them?" she replied.

I felt my face get hot as Joe raised his eyebrows, sighed, and then looked away. I realized I had done a bad, bad thing.

"What does the dog look like?" she asked.

"I'm not sure, it's so matted," I answered hesitantly, as my husband kicked me under the table. "Maybe a collie? Black and white. Some sort of shepherd mix?"

"Perfect," Jenny replied. "I can call both the shepherd rescue and the collie rescue. How old do you think it was?"

"Old," I said, shrugging. "It had a lot of gray on its face."

Jenny snapped her fingers. "Elderly rescue!" she cried.

The waitress brought over our coffee.

"You know, I wouldn't worry about it too much," I said, trying to spread some optimism. "The dog's been hanging out for who knows how long; it's getting food somewhere."

"So you think people are feeding it?" Jenny asked.

"Well, I wouldn't say that, but it found a can of refried beans in the trash that it was licking," I offered, saying anything I could think of to slow the quest down.

Joe did not look excited at all about the dog hunt. In fact, I think if this scenario had taken place two hundred years ago, he would have challenged my husband to a duel. And I need to say here that I had always known Joe to be a nice, patient guy, and I did not blame him one bit for being a little unenthusiastic about spending the day chasing a dirty dog that some stupid girl at breakfast had to open her big mouth about and spoil the lovely Sunday he had planned for himself. The dog, while not necessarily my problem, was my hang-up, and now I had opened the gates and let it run wild with Jenny and her dog-saving networks.

"We're going to have to take a cab back to Brooklyn. There's no way I can get a dog on the subway."

"It doesn't even have a leash," I stressed. "I don't know how you're going to get it to come to you."

"Don't eat all of your breakfast, Joe," Jenny advised. "We'll lure it."

"This sounds familiar," my husband said.

Jenny spent a good majority of brunch working the phone and calling every rescue group she could think of to see if she could find a place for the dog. Finally, one option looked hopeful, and I thought poor Joe was going to stab himself in the eye with a fork when Jenny, still on the phone, looked at him and asked, "How long do you think it would take for us if we got a cab to Long Island?"

With all of our breakfast leftovers boxed up, the four of us headed out of the restaurant and over to the apartment building on Bleecker. But once we got there, much to Joe's unrestrained glee, the dog was gone.

"It was right here," I said, pointing to the spot by the door, as if I was explaining to a news crew where I claimed to have seen Bigfoot selling knockoff purses out of a garbage bag. There was, again, no trace of the dog. I looked around the corner, then looked for the poop the dog had produced during our parting shot, and that was gone, too. Probably buried in the snow, I figured, and I sure wasn't going to go digging for it just to prove I had seen a mythical stray pooch that could appear and vanish at will.

Before I knew it, Joe was hailing a cab and we were waving goodbye, and then they drove away for Brooklyn, their whole day—the one I came within inches of detouring with matted fur—now before them.

With the exception of the fight I was pretty sure they were having in the taxi at that very moment.

On the day we left, we packed up our things, threw the left-overs away, and headed downstairs to hail a cab to the airport. We were alone in the elevator when it made a stop on a lower floor, and the doors opened to an older man with a very thin mustache.

"Can you make room for an old lady?" he said in a thick French accent, and smiled as he shuffled in to the elevator.

Oh, boy, I thought. What do you know? Dementia can give you a sex change even though you're the only one who feels it.

Then from behind him waddled a black-and-white tube of matted fur—part collie, part shepherd, I didn't know. But what I did know was what that dog looked like with its snout stuffed into a can of refried beans.

We rode the elevator the rest of the way in polite silence, mainly because if I opened my big mouth again about the hys-terically funny story of a decrepit, dirty dog that we kept seeing around the building and that my friend tried to save, I was most likely going to be riding to the airport alone.

The man walked to the vestibule of the lobby, opened the door, and the old lady sauntered out of the building as we fol-lowed behind.

The man smiled at us as we walked past, and we smiled back.

"She takes too long for me to stand out in that cold," he ex-plained, and then laughed.

We laughed, too, and kept laughing all the way into the cab, especially when I turned to take one more look at the dog as we pulled away and, in a pile of leftover snow, she was making her signature move on the side of the building.

Where Everyone Can
Hear You Scream

❧

I will do anything to prevent you from ringing my doorbell.
Honestly. I'm not fooling around.

If I see you heading toward my front door with your finger aimed at the doorbell, I'll fly off the couch like there's a
promise of a Mormon standing on my porch that I get to yell
at; I will open the door to my home dressed as a jiggly Jell-O
burrito, with a towel on my head and another one wrapped
around my girth; I will open the door after launching off the elliptical, dripping with sweat and sporting a yoga-pant cameltoe
that reaches upward of my waistband.

What I really should do is disconnect it, but I'm too afraid I
would hit a live wire and shoot across the street into the yard
of the neighbors that hate me. It doesn't make my situation any
better that I'm married to a guy who believes that turning off
the disposal and walking away from it when it makes a weird,
bone-crushing noise is the best option because, he believes, it
has the capacity to heal itself, given enough time. But that's
only if you don't watch it and, more important, don't interfere
with the order of the sink disposal by sticking your hand in it
to find the date pit that's been bouncing around in there, which
your wife found three seconds after you walked out of the

kitchen with the words "heal itself" still hanging in the air. So you see, silencing my doorbell is not an option and nowhere close to a reality, so there's no need to clutch on to that reverie.

The fact is that I'm stuck with a doorbell, and I'm stuck with a dog that emits a solar-flare version of a bark when she hears it. And that includes not only the real doorbell but door-bells on TV, the sudden appearance of a xylophone on a Big Band mix on my iPod, and anytime someone remotely unlocks a car that is anywhere on our block.

I truly can't do this bark justice with mere words; you have to experience in person the sharp, shrill pitch my dog is able to achieve to really absorb its power. Mariah Carey would seethe with jealousy, and she would lose the ability to sleep, knowing that a living, breathing creature out-screeched her by fathoms. Forget about run-of-the-mill eardrum-piercing pain; this bark has the potential to shatter your teeth and possibly pop out an eyeball. The only thing that I can equate it with is the sound an elderly woman would make if she believed she was being home-invaded and began running aimlessly through her house, confused, terrified, shrieking, and believing that death was mo-ments away. That's the sound my dog makes every single time someone rings that bell, even though it's just the mailman with a package for me from Spanx, which has a body shaper inside that's going to squeeze my inner organs so tight that my liver will poke out my nose.

"This has *got* to stop," my husband said after my dog nearly propelled both of us into cardiac arrest when she lost her shit during an episode of *The Closer*. "I just saw stars. There's something dripping down the side of my face. Is there blood coming out of my ear? Why does she do that? Why can't she have a regular *ruff-ruff* bark like other dogs her age?"

"God, I wish I knew," I said, wiping the spray of fruit punch

Crystal Light that had flown up onto my forehead and eyelashes after Maeby's bark stabbed my brain like a shard of glass. I wiped a far-flying droplet from the side of my husband's head. "Nothing bad has ever happened to her as a result of the doorbell ringing. If we had an idea of what freaks her out so much, maybe we could get her to stop."

And as if In Dog We Trust was listening to me from up above, the following week I got the new issue of *Bark,* a magazine about dogs, in the mail. Always excited to see it, I opened up the issue immediately and was doing a preliminary flip through when something caught my eye. It was an ad for a "dog translator," which said it could analyze my dog's barks, determine her emotion, and then deliver a sentence about what my dog's bark meant. It was touted as one of *Time* magazine's greatest inventions of the year. I wasted no time in going to the website and buying it right there on the spot.

Now, I know it seems foolish to believe in such a thing, especially considering that earlier that year I had swabbed the inside of my dog's mouth with a giant Q-tip, carefully placed it inside a sterile plastic tube, and mailed it off to get her DNA analyzed. And that wasn't the most ridiculous part of the equation. That had come when I went to the website and paid this DNA lab seventy-five dollars to send me the kit.

I need to explain here that I got my dog at the local pound, so her gene pool is rather murky, at best. She's fluffy, tan and white, and has one blue eye, one brown, and a speckled little nose. All paws pointed to Australian shepherd, that part was obvious, but it was the other half that had me wondering, especially when she was diagnosed with a form of lupus that affected her skin, nails, and that speckled little nose. If there was a breed that was more susceptible to that kind of illness and it could be identified, that might help prepare us for other directions the lupus might take in the future. Most likely, her mystery portion was golden retriever, but curiosity was eating away at me to find out for sure.

That reasoning aside, the truth of the matter is that I thought it would rock to have my dog's DNA tested, and I really am that kind of asshole who would write out a check for the amount of her weekly grocery budget in order to attain that bragging right.

But when I mentioned to the girls at the doggy day care how excited I was that I'd ordered the DNA kit, they advised me not to include a photo of my dog, as the kit encourages you to do, despite the claim that it's to attach to the photo area on your dog's Certificate of DNA when the results are returned to you. The girls informed me that according to their other clients—who were also apparently big enough assholes to write out seventy-five-dollar checks and rub a giant cotton swab all over their dogs' mouths—when the results came back, the dogs with photos enclosed were determined to be of lineage very much in line with their appearance. The kits that were returned sans photos, however, had results that were all over the map. A toy poodle was determined to be 50 percent German shepherd. A German shepherd was relayed to be 76 percent cocker spaniel. A corgi was actually a Siberian husky. I held back on the photo and trusted that we had not eaten spaghetti with butter for the last week in vain.

I have to say that, despite the reports of DNA testing run afoul, I still had hope when I ripped open the envelope that I wasn't a mark, a sucker, a rube, and that Maeby's heritage would be mapped out very clearly for me across the page. Sure enough, there it was, the document that detailed how my fluffy tan-and-white dog with her huge sweeping tail was mostly Doberman, and whatever part of her wasn't Doberman was boxer. After the report, I wasn't allowed to make any household decisions aside from blue or red Charmin for a very, very long time (and this may be insignificant to some, but we've been told that certain friends look forward to parties at our house because of the quality of our toilet paper. I'm not sure what that says about my snacks of celebration or hostess abilities, but if you want a smooth transaction after you've been drinking and eating finger foods, you know where to go).

But when I had to tell my husband that I'd ordered the dog translator, I knew things had to be different than they were with the DNA test.

"I think we might be able to crack the code of the hysterical bark," I insisted, showing him the ad as he frowned at the spaghetti dripping with butter that he'd twirled around his fork. "The website says that 'the Animal Emotion Analysis System analyzes the bark and determines the most accurate translation.' It's one of *Time* magazine's inventions of the year!"

When it arrived the following week via UPS, there was no containing me. I brought it into my office and dove into the package, ripping it apart like it was a meal. This magnificent invention—the one that was going to save me from answering the door armed with an apology every single time—was right at my fingertips and was anxious to help us reach a solution. The package came with an instruction booklet, which somehow flipped out of the box and slid under the elliptical machine, where I would have to get up to reach it.

Well, now, that's a shame, I thought as I looked at it for several seconds, knowing it was gone forever. "I bet that would have come in handy."

I moved on to the shiny red parts of the package, which looked like a little walkie-talkie, and then another small oval piece, which looked as if it had something of a microphone embedded in it. From the look of the box, the oval part slid onto the dog's collar, and the walkie-talkie was the receiver and translator.

I wasted no time and got right to work. I attached the microphone to Maeby's collar, put the receiver in front of me, and waited.

"Maeby," I commanded her. "Bark!"

Maeby looked at me for a moment, then put her head down and took a nap.

When my husband came home, I was very excited to show him our problem-solver, and he looked it over skeptically.

"How is this supposed to tell us what she's barking?" he asked.

"After she barks, it transmits to the walkie-talkie, and the translation pops up on that screen," I informed him.

"Does it work?"

"I don't know," I replied. "She hasn't barked all day. Everyone in the neighborhood and their dog has walked by our house today, but a little miss I know needed beauty sleep."

"So this expensive, useless thing doesn't work," my husband asserted. "So much for the Animal Emotion Analysis System."

"I didn't say that!" I cried, and snatched the walkie-talkie out of his undeserving hands. "She just hasn't been pulling her emotional end of the deal."

My husband went up to Maeby, who was still draped over the end of the couch, looking at us.

Quietly.

"Maeby, bark," my husband suggested.

She looked at him and then looked away, as if she was bored.

"Show her," I proposed. "Bark at her. Maybe that will encourage her."

"*Ruff!*" my husband said.

My dog was clearly insulted.

"Get closer to her, show her what you mean," I instructed.

My husband moved closer to Mae, leaned down by her little doggy head, and said, "*Ruff!*"

My dog responded by getting off the couch and moving in front of the fireplace.

My husband threw up his hands. I shrugged. And then I noticed that on the little screen of the walkie-talkie, something was being translated.

"You have a sad face," I informed him as I relayed what I saw on the screen. "The little dog in you said, 'I can't figure you out!'"

"Really?" my husband said, coming at me with his hand out. "It translated my bark?"

"Oh, oh," I said, pulling my arm away. "Now you're suddenly interested in my useless, expensive gadget."

"Come on," my husband said, reaching for it. "I wanna see."

"Here," I said, relenting and handing it over. I walked over to Maeby and scratched her ears, then kissed her little doggy head. "*Woooof!*"

"Wait . . . wait. . . ." my husband said, as if he was receiving signals from the International Space Station. "Oh, really? Is that what you think? It says, 'We're in trouble now!' And you have a smiley face."

"Ha-ha!!" I chortled. "You got that right!"

Mae got up and went back to the couch, where my husband bent down and barked rather loudly into her collar.

"'Where's my bone?' This is off. Maybe you have to calibrate it. I have no desire for a bone. And I'm still sad!" he read, as Mae climbed down off the couch again and tried to leave the room. "Maeby, stay! Maeby, stay! Oh, never mind."

He followed her down the hall and returned in a minute with Mae's collar in his hand. I have no idea where the dog went.

"*Woo-woo-woooo!*" he howled to the collar, and then laughed when he looked at the translator.

"What? Let me see," I said, reaching for the walkie-talkie, which had an angry face that pronounced, "Something's bothering me!"

"You are a moody pooch," I mocked, and grabbed the collar from him, then took a deep breath and released a "*Woooooooooooooooo!*" that would rival the call of any pack.

"Careful who you mess with!" the translator warned my husband.

Unfazed, he snatched the collar back and released a fierce bay of his own, as in "*Wooo-hooo-hooooooo!*"

"Please be nice to me," the translator said, and gave a frowny face.

"Hello, Omega!" I laughed when I read it. "Awwwww! Are the other doggies picking on you?"

"I am *not* the omega!" he insisted. "That is not what my call meant. My call was bold."

"Translator doesn't think so," I volleyed.

"It's wrong," he insisted. "That was definitely an alpha call. I did an alpha call!"

"Well," I offered. "Maybe you were an alpha barking in Chinese."

"*A-wooooooo!*" my husband barked into the collar.

"And the survey says . . . 'Please be nice to me.' Again," I said, with an odd look. "You are one pathetic, insecure dog, my friend."

"I don't believe you," my husband said, pulling the translator from my hand to read for himself. "It may have been the call of a lone wolf, but it was *not* pathetic. And there you go. It was a wolf call, that's why. It was clearly wolf. This translates Dog. Not Wolf. Apparently it's not trans-species."

He then emitted a rather ferocious bark, during which I was surprised that spittle didn't fly from his jowls and that he retreated from the translator without leaving bite marks on it.

"Was that a wolf or a chupacabra?" I asked. "We don't need to fight over the translator. It's a walkie-talkie, not the hindquarters of an elk."

"But it's not understanding me," my husband said.

"Can't you see how frustrated I am?" the translator relayed. Angry face.

"Really?" I asked him. "Because I think this walkie-talkie could easily work at the United Nations."

"No," my husband insisted. "It's broken. It's clearly off. Maybe we need new batteries for it."

"Maybe it just needs time to heal," I suggested.

And then I saw a shadow pass by the front door, and before I could put on my cameltoe pants, rip off a bra, or become soaking wet, the first note of the mailman ringing the doorbell hit the air. This was followed immediately by the frantic scratching of lupus dog toes clawing wood floors, as Maeby came around the corner into the living room like a hillbilly with a pit crew and a sponsorship from Walmart.

And there was no preparing for it. The bark, high and shrill and real, sliced through the living room like a machete through a block of government cheese. My husband and I both winced as she charged through her excruciating symphony, her dagger bark so painful it reached up and punched me in my sinuses.

Then, as soon as it shot out of her mouth, it ended once she realized it was Dave, the postman, who is her best friend.

"Wait . . ." my husband said, staring at the translator. "I'm getting something, I'm getting something . . ."

I bent in closer to see.

And there, on the screen, in response to Maeby's bark, was "We're having fun now!" and a big, fat smiley face.

My husband and I looked at each other.

He was the first one to say it.

"Oh, my Dog," he mumbled quietly. "That's her *happy* noise."

"We're in trouble now," I replied, almost in a whisper.

"Please be nice to me," my husband barely added.

I'm Touched

"Just relax," Brandie said, as she reached forward to give me a hand massage. "This is going to be fun."

It was the first time I had been to this particular salon to get my hair done, and when Brandie, the colorist, was done applying the color, she informed me that as part of the salon service I could either have a hand massage while we waited to wash my hair out or I could have my makeup consultation.

Now, the last time I had my makeup done was the day I got married, and I walked out of that salon looking less like a girl who was about to snag a cute boy for the rest of her life and more like an undercover cop who was about to go stand out in front of a cheap motel and arrest ministers. All I needed was a fur vest and a chipped eyetooth. So I wisely passed on the dolling-up and chose the hand massage instead, because I'd never had one.

I limply presented my paw, which Brandie took and started . . . massaging. I tried my best to ignore it.

"Just relax your hand," Brandie said calmly.

"Okay," I said with a little laugh.

"Are you relaxing it?" she asked me.

"I am," I replied.

"Because it doesn't feel relaxed," she hinted.

"I'm very relaxed," I said with a nod and a smile.

She kept doing more massaging things.

"Juuuuuust relax; let your hand go limp," she said softly.

"I did," I let her know.

She looked up at me and smiled, but even I could see that my hand looked like I had pulled it from a freezer covered by tarps in the basement of a clown's house. And, honestly, that's about as limp as I go.

"Maybe we should stop," I suggested, pulling my hand lightly at first, then tugging harder, then finally yanking.

"See? It's cool!" I said very cheerily. "Thank you very much. That was nice."

"Okay," Brandie said, a bit alarmed at my aggressive limb recall. "Would you like to play with some eye shadow?"

"Maybe I should have magazine time now," I suggested.

"That's a great idea," she said, a little too eagerly.

As soon as my hair was done and I got in the car to go home, I called my sister.

"You wouldn't believe what just happened," I said as soon as she answered. "I freaked out over someone giving me a hand massage. I was forced to do that or play with makeup."

"Was this some sort of beauty mugging?" she asked. "Are you in L.A.? You'd better check your boobs. They could have gotten six sizes bigger before you even knew what was happening."

"No, no, no, I was getting a touch-up on my roots and it's part of the service," I explained. "I could either get a hand massage or I could get my makeup done. So I let someone touch my hand. It was a mistake."

"You're telling *me*!" she exclaimed. "Remember when I went on that business trip to South Carolina at that fancy resort? I decided to get a massage, because I thought it would be fun and that I deserved it because I just had a baby. Fun? A stranger touching me all over? No one deserves that!"

Apparently, as soon as the massage began, my sister knew she was in trouble and tried to drop hints to the masseuse that it just wasn't her thing.

"I told her I was ticklish," my sister said. "So instead of it ending, she put lotion on me for an hour, which turned a regular old massage into a stranger caressing me. Moistly."

"I'm establishing a 'safe' word if strangers ever want to touch me again," I said. *"Blueberry! Blueberry!"*

"No kidding," my sister agreed. "I gave birth faster than it took that hour to pass. Mistake? When I finally got back to my room, I felt like I'd just been involved in a long-term relationship with a sixty-year-old Yugoslavian lady. I apologized to my husband for weeks."

Notaros, at least in our dynasty, are not huggers. We're not touchers, patters, or embracers. We're flinchers, jerkers, and recoilers. We like a loooooot of space. Honestly, I don't think that being able to lift up my arms and do one copter rotation without having my elbow in someone's mouth is really asking all that much. We do best in that environment. When our physical security boundaries are breached, the issue will be dealt with swiftly and mercilessly. If you creep up behind me in a checkout line and the alarm is sounded, I will be forced to ask if you intend to crawl up my ass, because that's clearly where you're heading. If you persist, I may have no choice but to challenge you to a kicking fight in the parking lot.

This has been awkward, however, because I married into a touching family that has no problem walking by one another in a galley kitchen, picking a stray leaf out of one another's hair, or reaching over and wiping a smear of jelly or peanut butter off a sibling's cheek. In my family, the game of "There. No, *there*," is so prevalent that we played it for prizes one year at my nephew's birthday. It lasted for so long that he burst into tears, wiped his face off with a paper towel, and left everyone in the dynasty without bragging rights.

"What's going on here?" I asked the first time I saw my then to-be husband and his mother say goodbye, a hug that lasted longer than some sitcoms. "It was like you were going off to war."

My husband shrugged. "The lady likes to hug" was all he said, and I had no choice but to wonder what made his family skin-friendly and mine skin-averse.

Then one night when I was on the treadmill watching *Nova*, thrilled that it was an episode I could understand, and my husband was in the living room watching the same thing. It was about scientists in Montreal who were studying the epigenome and how it was built to respond to experiences around us. Not only does the epigenome respond, but experience itself, it turns out, actually changes it by turning genes on and off. The scientists tested their theory out with two types of rats: mothers who licked and groomed their offspring after birth, and mothers who didn't. The results showed that the offspring of the licking mothers were good at mazes, had calm demeanors, and didn't eat all of the candy in the bowl. The mothers who drank coffee, smoked cigarettes, and talked on the phone all the time had offspring who were anxious, blew at puzzles, and got chunky because they couldn't leave the jelly beans alone.

I can't even tell you if I turned the treadmill off, because the next thing I knew, I was in the hallway, where I almost crashed into my husband.

"I had a non-licking mother!" I cried.

"You had a non-licking mother!" he yelled.

Suddenly it all made sense. The hand-yanking. The anxiety. The Pooh shirt. The aversion to tall walls and sharp corners. The challenges to parking-lot kicking fights. All of the symptoms now came together. I had a non-licking mother, my genes had been turned off as a result, and I was nothing more than an anxiety-filled, jelly-bean-eating lab rat who couldn't stand to be touched, even for free.

So it made sense to me that if my environment had turned my genes off, maybe I could get them to go back on. I decided to take it slow at first and try out some hugging. I hugged my neighbor Louise, after her dog died, and that went really well. I hugged my friend Jim after I hadn't seen him in fifteen years and we met for dinner during Christmas vacation. Now, I want to make it clear that I was still very much at a beginning-hugger level; I was taking it slow and trying not to move too fast. I was not embracing, by any means. Hugs that had time parameters, like One-Mississippi Hugs. I gave out a couple more, although I couldn't actually say they were changing my life and making me more of a licked rat. I was keeping it safe, keeping it in the family, so to speak, until one day when I got a little hug-cocky.

I was visiting Seattle for a couple of days and met a friend for coffee while I was there. We had both attended a creative-writing conference a year earlier; I got to know her and her husband and thought both were very cool, very nice people. We had a great time talking and drinking wine and I really enjoyed their company.

So I was thrilled when she said she had the afternoon free during my visit. We met and walked to a little café. As we were taking the last bites of our chocolate chip cookies a couple of hours later, it began to rain heavily, and just then my friend's phone rang. It was her husband, who offered, very nicely, to come and pick us up so I wouldn't have to walk back to my hotel in a downpour.

Now, that's sweet, right? Isn't that thoughtful and kind? That's exactly what I was thinking, because even though I didn't have that long of a walk, maybe a mile, I would have gotten soaked. As we pulled up to the front of the hotel, all of this was running through my mind, and certainly this met the parameters of a One-Mississippi Hug. No, I decided, just go for the handshake. Don't get ahead of yourself. You're not ready.

You're not ready!

And I was firmly comfortable with my decision about the handshake or the wave as the car pulled to a stop. But the next thing I knew, I was reaching across the front of the car with my arms open toward the driver's seat—although my momentum came to a sudden and jarring halt because I had neglected to take off my seat belt. Once I had been jerked back to reality, like I was in a log on Splash Mountain and someone quickly applied the brakes, I knew this had been a terrible choice, but I was in it now. There was no getting out; there was no abandoning the mission. You just can't open your arms to someone, change your mind, and high-five them instead. Once freed from my restraints, I had no choice but to go back in and deliver a second attempt, but I hadn't come close to mastering the art of positioning. Going in from the side angle, and basically lying over the console, I got my right arm around him but my left arm got all squished up against the side of the driver's seat like a flipper, which I realized was moving wildly, as if I was patting him on the back with both hands, all while my friend watched the whole thing from the middle of the backseat. When I eventually retreated, it was clear that not only had he gotten a face-full of my slightly damp hair but that I had administered a Five-Mississippi Hug, and it was probably one of the Most Inappropriate Hugs on record (that was not given at a funeral to the person in the casket).

I'm not the only one in my family to breach the touching protocol, either, by the way. My father staged a coup around 2000 and started to kiss people hello and goodbye on the cheek, a move that I could only assume was generated on a trip to Italy. We all just tried to take it very lightly and not get too worked up about it, since they were basically air kisses; he also put up a red, white, and green sign in his garage that said, PARKING FOR ITALIANS ONLY. He was clearly feeling the Motherland. We sort of brushed it off when he started incorporating the Psych Hug, which was putting his hand on our shoulder right before leaning in for the kiss. Not a full hug, but just enough of a wrestling move that you couldn't easily get away without collapsing or igniting a jet pack.

Then, in 2003, when my soon-to-be-brother-in-law, Greg, started hanging around, my father introduced The Double, which took the foundation of the kiss and the Psych Hug and added another kiss—that's right, twins—to the mix. For a short time, he only gave Greg The Double. Being new, Greg had no reason to believe that anything was out of the ordinary in this culture, thinking we just hadn't assimilated completely yet, since it was clear that his kind wasn't allowed to park in the garage. Sensing no opposition, my dad then started working it in among the rest of us without a briefing or warning, and on one occasion my husband thought he had fulfilled his departing requirement with the single kiss, only to be caught off guard when my dad went in for The Double and kissed my husband square on the lips.

Everyone saw it; everyone looked away.

The silence in the car on the way home was disturbing.

"I'm sorry," I finally said weakly. "I thought I told you he had revised the kiss and was now making double contact. I thought you knew. He's been doing it to Greg for a while."

"I have no idea what you are talking about," my husband answered staunchly. "I have never kissed your dad on the lips."

And no one has talked of it since.

After the Five-Mississippi Hug, I stopped. But, you know, I'm a little glad that hugging didn't really work out for me. As a family of non-lickers, we are decidedly fine the way we are. We are very happy. So what if we can't get a massage without feeling dirty and shameful? I never had one before the anxious-hand incident, and it turns out I'm not missing out on anything I can't live without. I know Brandie is clean, but my sister didn't know where those Yugoslavian hands had been. Who knew what unclean body she was rubbing lotion on just an hour before?

And so what if I was the offspring of a non-licking mother? With one lick, who knew where I would have ended up? I might have been the one coming at someone's thigh with two hands full of lotion.

Seeing *Nova* actually reinforced what I had suspected: I'd have a boring, nicely balanced life and have a boring, nicely balanced job, and I wouldn't see any of the things I see on a daily basis that licked people can't see. The licking mothers, I think, were boring mothers who never wanted to shave their grandsons' armpits when they hit puberty or emailed their daughters warnings that wearing ponytails was basically putting a handle on your head and nearly guaranteeing an abduction. Their boring offspring would never get banned from the post office because she got snotty about stamps, or banned from a party because she mouthed the words to a song, or became trapped in a shirt in a fancy store because the jelly beans made her arms enormous (not because she's strong).

I'll bet we laugh harder at family gatherings, once we determine who the scapegoat is going to be. We have a lot more stuff to talk about than how calm we were that day and how it didn't even annoy us when the lady in front of us in line at FedEx/Kinko's picked up her copies and then asked the clerk if they knew someplace close by where she could ship them. I am delighted that no one has ever opened a family dinner at my mother's house with the phrase "I solved the most fantastic maze today!" Not to mention that I like getting checks and impersonal gift cards for birthdays and Christmas, not subscriptions to the Fig of the Month Club or a book of Sudoku puzzles.

I know I wouldn't have ended up being me, and my sisters wouldn't have ended up being them. Could you imagine if I just smeared my face with Mexican-smuggled Retin-A that expired four years ago, and my mother looked across the kitchen table to tell me how great my skin looked, instead of telling me that I just gave myself face-wide melanoma? I would have no choice but to burst into tears immediately and cry, "Why are you so boring? Jesus! Stop licking me!"

I like my family just the way it is, and if I had to pick a Licked Laurie or a Non-Licked Laurie, I'd go with the latter, of course (with the option to have fewer moles and fill in the bald spot). My mother taught me never to buy green beans after a lady with too much boob showing has touched them. That's valuable advice not all nine-year-olds get. I still use it to this day, only now it applies to hippies and the food they bring to potlucks.

My husband concurs, because a licked person would never agree to crabwalk around the backyard as a form of marital exercise; test the old wives' tale that earlobes are in exact alignment with your nipples (not on me, over shirt, and ruled completely false); follow an email from him to meet him in the living room in five minutes for a balancing contest (only then to have him make fun of my choice of balancing position, which he said was "too American" and that it "didn't even *mean* anything" because I had my leg up, toe pointed forward, my arms up at about forty-five-degree angles, and my fingers were apparently pointing, too. WTF ever. I won); or agree that you should change the name of your canine companion to Doggy McPushy because she believes I am the guest in the bed at night.

"When you say 'Doggy McPushy' with a cough drop in your mouth," my husband just informed me, "it takes on an entirely different meaning."

"A licker would never get that joke," I replied.

"I like you just the way you are, but it would be nice if you could leave some jelly beans for someone else," he said, coming in for a hug, to which I felt forced to immediately throw my hands up and cry,

"Blueberry!!"

Acknowledgments

Thank you to the readers out there for your great letters, your hilarious posts, and your crazy comments, and for keeping in touch with me, but most of all for reading: I can't do what I do unless you do what you do. Even Steven. You guys never fail to make my day, every day.

Thank you to Jenny Bent, who let me tell the tale of the French dog after many, many years; Pamela Cannon, who expertly poked at this manuscript like a coroner, polished it, and got it ready to take to market; Beth Pearson, who rightfully questioned every suspicious comma; and Brian McLendon and Diana Franco who pushed it like good drugs.

As always, mountains of gratitude to the guy I married, who can make me laugh faster than anybody on the planet and will let me dork out in strange and unpredictable ways without calling a doctor to Frances Farmer me. Who knew I was capable of making a good choice? And thanks to my family and friends: keep doing what you're doing. I'm still collecting material for the next book, you know.

Additionally, I have copious amounts of humble gratitude for Jody Lucas, who unwittingly shared the story of her friend, Lucy Fisher, with me, which set the stage for *Spooky Little Girl*. I'd also like to thank her for not scolding me as loudly as she could for my resistance to flossing, and for handing over enough free toothpaste, toothbrushes, and teeth picks to make a girl with bleeding gums smile. I hope I did her friend Lucy justice, especially since when we meet, Jody is armed with pointy, sharp metal objects headed for my mouth.

And finally, many thanks to Kelly Kulchak and Kathy White for their support, notes, and for driving me around when it's 113 degrees in L.A.

Many, many thanks,
Laurie

ABOUT THE AUTHOR

LAURIE NOTARO has disproportionately chubby arms, which once helped her save the life of her best friend, who was trapped in a wheelchair and choking on a quiche. She has fought a size M shirt in a dressing room (she lost), has been banned from the local post office for wanting too many stamps, and has burned her neck on several occasions by trying to get out of a car too quickly without releasing the seat belt first. In third grade, she sucked a fly up her nostril. It died and several classmates screamed. She now lives with her husband and dog in a small house, and when something tickles her nose, she has learned to breathe out instead of in.